VEILS OF DISTORTION

"Think you know a 'fake' news story when you see one? As Zada cogently shows, the way the brain works makes that highly unlikely. This is a powerful dissection of why we get bamboozled by the stories we are fed, and a guide to what we can do about it."

— DENISE WINN, AUTHOR OF *THE MANIPULATED MIND: BRAINWASHING, CONDITIONING AND INDOCTRINATION*

"As we spend ever more of our lives staring at screens, it can be hard to remember that our daily existence is not consumed by natural disasters, shootings, celebrity indiscretions, and apocalyptic politics. What is this realm of horrors and trivialities and how did it colonize our perception? Drawing on long experience as a newsroom insider, John Zada illuminates the unseen and subtle dynamics by which mind, medium, and professional practice amalgamate into 'the news.' *Veils of Distortion* offers a brilliant primer on how the form of an industry gave rise to our dominant picture of reality, and in some cases to reality itself."

— GREG JACKSON, JOURNALIST AND AUTHOR OF *PRODIGALS* AND "VICIOUS CYCLES: THESES ON A PHILOSOPHY OF NEWS"

"John Zada has shared a passionate, insider's account of how "churnalism" is bad not just for those who produce the news, but for everyone who consumes it. Of all the injuries that beset the world, few are as self-inflicted as our surrender to false narratives that are the *sine qua non* of today's media barrage. Better to ignore it all, or as Zada hopefully urges, *do something*—each and every one of us—before it's too late."

— IAN GILL, JOURNALIST AND AUTHOR OF *NO NEWS IS BAD NEWS: CANADA'S MEDIA COLLAPSE— AND WHAT COMES NEXT*

VEILS OF DISTORTION

ALSO BY JOHN ZADA

In the Valleys of the Noble Beyond: In Search of the Sasquatch

VEILS OF DISTORTION

HOW THE NEWS MEDIA WARPS OUR MINDS

JOHN ZADA

TERRA INCOGNITA

Visit the author's website at:

johnzada.com

For everyone

Our means of apprehending reality determine the reality we apprehend. What few could foresee was that, as technological and business pressures drew the news further toward stimulation and away from representing immediate life, at a certain point the value of the news' being true, its hewing as close as possible to an accurate picture of the world, would fall away.

– Greg Jackson, "Vicious Cycles: Theses on a Philosophy of News"

Man is the child of his customs, not the child of his ancestors.

– Ibn Khaldun, 14th century Arab philosopher in *The Muqaddimah*

CONTENTS

PREFACE

Around the time I signed up for my first television news writing job over a decade ago with the newly launched CBC News Network in Toronto, I started noticing a trend across society: people were tuning out of news coverage in droves. Every time I met someone new and the subject of my job came up they would tell me matter-of-factly that they recently made the decision to stop consuming news. "Oh, I don't watch the news anymore. It's way too gloomy," one person said. "The news media instills fear and hatred in us," quipped another. People were often tired, or fed up, with the negativity and pessimism of news coverage and felt that 'the world' the news was portraying didn't equate with their living experience of it. Others told me they felt emotionally manipulated for ratings, subscriptions and clicks to the point where their wellness was being negatively impacted. Some even held the deep conviction that the news stoked, or amplified, the chaos in the world. Those sentiments reached a crescendo during the COVID-19 pandemic, when news operations went into full-throttle to churn out as many daunting stories as they could on a daily basis without taking stock of the consequences for society. To safeguard their already strained mental and physical health, nearly everyone I know made a calculated decision to largely tune out of the unrelenting coverage.

Whatever our exact opinions, many of us feel that news cycles in the West, especially in North America, have turned into spectacles of imbecility. News organizations, which have seen their advertising revenue streams reduced to a trickle by the internet, have doubled-down in their pursuit of emotive sensation with the desperation of a drowning person grasping for a life raft. This tireless attempt to win and hold audiences resorts to the same old methods which have sent so many news consumers packing in the first place. Donald Trump was brought front-and-centre in this effort; indeed, the phenomenon of his coming to power in the first place is not inextricable from the calculating and excessive media coverage of his belly flop into politics in the run-up to the 2016 U.S. election.

But the madness gripping the news media goes beyond Trump's erstwhile presidency. Every contentious issue and debate is now seized upon—whether about politics, race, identity, or gender—and thrown into a coliseum where its partisans brawl like professional wrestlers in front of cheering and jeering audiences who later continue those battles online, and sometimes on the street. The elevation of local crime stories, celebrity scandals and social media tiffs to dramas of national and international importance also figures in this new campaign to agitate and entertain the masses. Hardly a day goes by when we aren't blindsided by stories so bizarre and unlikely, so irresistibly morbid at times, that truth and fiction seem to swap positions like magnetic poles that have flipped:

—TEENAGE BOY DIES OF BUBONIC PLAGUE AFTER EATING MARMOT

—BANGLADESH 'TREE MAN' WANTS HANDS AMPUTATED TO RELIEVE PAIN

—GRETA THUNBERG LOOK-ALIKE IN YUKON GOLD RUSH PHOTO SPARKS ONLINE FRENZY

—DOCTORS REMOVE LIVE WORM FROM WOMAN'S TONSIL

—WOMAN DETAINED AFTER VIDEO APPEARS TO SHOW HER THROWING OWN FECES AT TIM HORTONS STAFF

There seems to be no end to these circus shows offered up by a once more respectable profession now co-opted into the entertainment industrial complex to such a degree that it has become a surreal parody of itself. The problem is not that these reported events aren't happening—they are. We live in a strange world that is undergoing greater and more rapid change than at any other time in recorded history, and in which nearly anything that happens can be documented by ad-hoc citizen reporters. But what we don't learn from the news—because its doyens either won't tell us, or can't because they don't realize it—is that the events it covers tend to be outliers: they are exceptions and not the rule. The choice of stories and the extent of the coverage and significance attributed to them are not reflective of most of our day-to-day experiences. By featuring them as they do, the news creates a distorted picture of our reality. Ironically, by implying that the world they depict *is* the world we physically inhabit every day, the news threatens to catalyze a self-fulfilling prophecy by way of our manipulated reactions. By defining reality, even inadvertently, they can thereby alter it.

This, I suspect, is part of the reason why so many people have tuned the news out: most of us want no part in this make-believe charade.

The recurring feedback I've received from friends, family and strangers (and in exceptionally rare cases, work colleagues), combined with my own up-close observations and realizations about the news business, has prompted me to try to explain the less visible components of media distortion from a bigger picture perspective. The compulsion to do so is compounded by an unsettling silence from within the industry. With the exception of a handful of journalists (some of whom I quote here), very few people working in the business share their experiences with the public—even after retiring from their jobs or switching careers. News bosses almost never solicit big picture feedback—of the kind I include in this work—from their staff. One of the most important discussions of our age, rivalling in significance any issue that the news might cover, is not taking place. What is this strange creature we call 'the news'? And how many of our societal ills are created, and made worse, by it?

In this book I use general terms like 'news media,' 'news industry' and 'the news' to describe a wider industry bound by a common work culture, practices and goals. At the same time, I do not mean to imply a monolithic entity. News organizations are made up of different people who vary in talent, motivation, integrity, vision and quality of work. This book is not about the faults of any particular individuals, not an anarchist-style rant from a disenchanted news hack, not a conspiracy-minded manifesto, and certainly not a call to end all news. Nor does it reflect any political or ideological slant—the practises described here operate across partisan divides.

Instead, it's about an industry's *work culture* and its relationship to the wider *societal culture* which it both reflects and impacts, looked at through sociological, psychological and anthropological lenses. The book draws more upon my experiences and observations working in cable TV news, but also addresses to a lesser extent other media as well: print, online and radio news—all of which are converging in the digital realm. *Veils of Distortion* is an attempt to shed light on the systemic automation of human beings at the heart of the contemporary news machine in order to help us better understand how news is produced, the prisms and filters that distort it, and how it affects us, so that we're not helpless pawns; and so that we don't feel we have to disconnect from it completely and thereby throw-out the baby with the bathwater, as many people have done.

I strongly believe that we have to understand how falsehood manifests in the mainstream news media—before it undermines individuals and societies irrevocably.

PART I

VEILS OF DISTORTION

Much smoke has been seen, and caused great fear of fire–even when no fire ensued.

– Middle Eastern proverb

THE NEWS AS DISTORTION

OF ALL THE expressions coined in the maelstrom of change in the early 21st century, none has captured the confusion and uncertainty of our disordered state of affairs like the term "fake news." The Collins Dictionary, which included "fake news" in its 2017 Word of the Year list alongside "echo chamber," "gig economy," and "fidget spinner," defines it as "false, often sensational, information disseminated under the guise of news reporting." Generally regarded as a form of propaganda meant to promote or discredit a public figure, political movement or company, fake news is also considered to be a branch of cyberwarfare and is widely thought to have upended the American election of 2016. Its peril is deemed so great that the Bulletin of Atomic Scientists kept the Doomsday Clock at two minutes to midnight at the start of 2019 on account of it—despite the easing of tensions between the United States and North Korea that should have otherwise turned back its minute-hand. The sowing of online propaganda and disinformation today comes as little surprise to the few prescient naysayers, who, at the dawn of the Internet Age, foresaw the dangers of a technology that allowed anyone to publish anything they pleased.

But is 'fake news' really the omnipresent menace it is claimed to be? How much of what most of us actually engage with online everyday fits that exact definition?[1]

To be sure, the term itself, like so many other catchphrases, has become overhyped. Fake news is a trope so used and abused, both in truth and deceit, that it can now refer to virtually anything. As one writer describes, "It [fake news] has become a vehicle for expressing our hostility, similar to yelling 'boo' at a sports game." Research suggests that "fake news" is less common, attractive, viral and influential than originally believed. In the 2016 U.S. election only a slim demographic was exposed to, and shared articles from, fake news domains: mostly conservative and elderly voters, especially those who were largely pro-Trump in orientation. Aric Toler, a researcher who tracks Russian disinformation operations, told *The New Yorker* recently that, if anything, mainstream media coverage of Russian fake news operations has the effect of magnifying their reach beyond anything Moscow could achieve by itself. "The tiny whimper of disinformation is transformed into something far louder and more dangerous," he says. Our obsession with it helps to fulfill its mission.

There is a far bigger danger, however, that arises from the *use* of the term fake news; one that is nearly invisible, unmentioned, and which renders society vulnerable in a different way: **the implication that, just because there is such a thing as "fake news" all news that is not designated fake is therefore "real."**

Falsehood exists in degrees. It occupies a spectrum, and is

determined by any number of intentions and actions, both conscious and unconscious. Corporate news operations of the "real news" variety have always been prone to certain habits that can, at the very least, tinge reporting with some degree of falsehood that has consequences. For instance, when the news takes a perpetually aggressive stance towards all politicians, making every personal or political gaffe or misstep into as large a scandal as possible, they generate cynicism and antagonism in our leaders (and in the wider political establishment), frightening them, and increasing secrecy, paranoia and belligerence on their part—rather than transparency.

Thus, an important distinction needs to be made. "Fake news" is designed to trick you and involves stories deliberately made up to go viral. They are conscious deception operations. When I speak about falsehood in mainstream news, by contrast, I am referring to the more oblique, often inadvertent falsehoods that combine in piecemeal and collude with our perceptions to infect our overall picture of reality.

It's easy to forget that mass media news outlets are run by imperfect humans working as part of an insular professional culture with its own idiosyncratic habits, workflows and agendas that inevitably transform and distort information as prisms do light. So I'm not just talking about the factual inaccuracy of any given story, or the corporate biases that Chomsky and Herman describe in their classic *Manufacturing Consent*. It is also the impacts *upon* information through its commercial and mechanized processing. These include flawed human assumptions, perceptions and workflows in the newsroom that result in a society-wide phenomenon of "broken telephone." These and other factors twist, bend and shape real events to create a caricature of the world *which our brains can then process only too easily, as they evolved to simplify reality*. Our limited ability as consumers to properly verify and contextualize the news distorts it even further.

I contend therefore that, as far as threats go at present, what we call "fake news" pales in comparison to this largely unintentional falsehood in the mainstream news. We engage with the products of the latter infinitely more. Its machinery is more deeply embedded in our culture. And the process of distortion that it engenders occurs largely below mental awareness—and is thus much harder to pinpoint or identify than fake news.

There are numerous warping layers, "veils of distortion" as I call them, most of them invisible, that interpose their skewing effect at manifold points in the communication process between news producer and news consumer. That is what we are going to look at first.

WHY WE'RE DUPES FOR NEWS

If you look at the way the news media report the world, you will see that they do not, for instance, say: 'The big news in Europe this evening is that 240 million people had a pleasant, quiet dinner at home.' In fact, most evenings that is the major story. Yet, when was the last time anybody said that on the news? In the same way, the mind is not organized to tell you what's actually going on, but rather is organized to tell you what you need to act on next.

    – Robert Ornstein, *MindReal*

NEW IS the root of the word 'news.' Hard news elevates and fetishizes the new. People who work in the news industry are not in the business to tell you what happened last year, last month or even last week—unless it is a *new* revelation about an otherwise older event. News organizations make their money by grabbing and holding your attention with novel and unexpected happenings unfolding *now* while phasing-out what came just before. This is the fundamental imperative repeatedly drilled into every neophyte and veteran news employee. And it's what differentiates hard news from more conscientious and slower-moving current affairs, magazine and long-form journalism. News producers extract and package the new with such tenacity and consistency because there is a niche market for it: new information is prioritized and fast-tracked into human consciousness. We are hyper-sensitive to news.

The human brain evolved to register dramatic and sudden events in our environment because these tended, more often than not, to be the most threatening and deadly. Wild carnivores, erupting volcanoes and hostile tribes found exceptional receptivity in our awareness. Our survival depended on being able to quickly recognize and react to these dangers. It's why we have a morbid fascination with and give a disproportionate amount of attention to stories of terror attacks, murders, plane crashes, natural disasters and riots. It's also why, given the chance, the news will feature these stories and allot them premium real estate in their coverage. These stories grab and hold the attention of the public, thereby monetizing it.

The inverse is also said to be the case: good news is no news.

In his book *MindReal*, the late American psychologist and author, Robert Ornstein writes that the brain's main shortcut to survival is to compare new stimulus in our environment with what came *before*—and to determine which changes need reacting to. "A sensory change," Ornstein writes, "is a difference in stimulus from one moment to the next. One sensation always follows and precedes another, so one stimulus is louder, softer, brighter, dimmer, warmer, colder, greener or redder than something else. We compare relative differences between stimuli." We are extraordinarily sensitive to new and recent information. Any physical movement caught in our peripheral vision, however small, is brought to awareness. By comparison, when stimulus becomes constant in our environment, it is habituated in the mind. We tune it out. Whether it is the sound of an old refrigerator droning, the boisterous street traffic of Bombay, or a radio playing in the background, it soon becomes invisible to us.

Our minds, conversely, are tuned to news. We're dupes for it. It's why the judgement of news producers leans towards the shocking, the sensational, the bizarre, the lurid and the unexpected. It's also why, barring the availability of new stories, rolling 24-hour TV news producers, often with the vehemence of construction site foremen, constantly demand news be kept looking like new—even if it's not. The tiniest information is added, stories re-worded, details re-ordered and newer footage swapped for the old, to make the news *appear* less recognizable than when it ran before, all to keep it as "new" as possible—and to increase its shelf life. Whether they know it or not, their job is to grab us with whatever material best mimics those ancient changes in our environment that were once threatening.

By contrast, less dramatic, and slower moving stories seldom make the editorial cut in big news organizations—there isn't an evolutionary necessity to pay attention to news about a decrease in China in the demand for elephant ivory. Or that Paraguay recently became the first Latin American country to entirely eradicate malaria. Similarly, stories that once commanded our attention, like the Syrian civil war, tend to disappear from coverage over time as they become regularly reported and constantly buzz in our ears. We evolved to tune out continuous noise. It no longer shocks us and prompts us to be vigilant. It's old news.

THE FILTER

The news of the day comprises real and pseudo-events and even, sometimes, real news, but it is only one of infinite possibilities of how we might narrativize the world. It strives to be factual but adheres to strict conventions of format about what can and can't appear. It collapses the dimensionality we rely on to judge the world around us so that the proportions of the world it presents cannot agree with the proportions of our lives—"cannot" because the news is above all else this proportionality, this idiosyncratic condensation of the world out there.

– Greg Jackson, "Vicious Cycles: Theses on a Philosophy of News"

THERE ARE many criteria that determine what constitutes news and what makes the cut on any given news day: from how old a story is, to which other news organizations (and how many) are reporting it, to whether there are accompanying images, videos or sound clips, to how well-known (or not) its protagonist and location are, to whether the story personally interests journalists. Layers of decision-making are devoted to cherry-picking events from a vast ocean of goings-on around the world. Choices can come days or weeks in advance from the lofty heights of senior management with no direct connection to the newsroom to the lowly depths of the unpaid newsroom intern who points out a breaking story which others have missed. This filtering results in neatly curated packages that appear in print and online, and in radio and TV broadcasts: daily snapshots of our world composed of a handful of events. This creates an impression that the stories appearing in the news must therefore be the most important; that they are the brick-and-mortar of history, even. It also implies that our world—and its state of affairs—is merely the sum of what makes the news.

Yet nothing could be further from the truth.

Twentieth century Polish-American scholar Alfred Korzybski championed the idea—known in other times and places—that humans do not experience objective reality. He claimed that what we know and see of the external world is that which has reached us after being filtered through the brain. "The world is not an illusion, it is an abstraction," Korzybski once wrote.

His most famous and oft-quoted maxim "the map is not the territory" is a distillation of all his ideas in this regard. What he meant is that our mental abstractions and representations of a terrain, no matter how detailed or well-constructed, do not resemble the real thing. Rather, our maps are grossly inaccurate. They are at best metaphors. The Argentinian writer Jorge Luis

Borges borrowed this idea for a piece of short fiction he wrote entitled *On Exactitude in Science*, in which he imagines a map that corresponds *exactly* in size and scale with the terrain it describes. One implicit message of Borges' story is that the only truly precise map *is the territory itself*.

This map-terrain relation applies to the news, which we can regard as the most basic and crude "map" that depicts the event-scape of the world. Were it to be accurate, such a map would have to represent as many events as possible, both in proportion and in relation to one another, including the negative space of "non-events" and the otherwise invisible currents of cause-and-effect that link them all. Instead, what we get with the news is a handful of stories, some more important, others less important, many unimportant, which are fished from a wider ocean of goings-on, and are arranged in a way that says: "This is the world as it exists today."

Of course, it is anything but.

Like the images projected on the wall of Plato's cave—it is reality caricatured. An abbreviated *re*-presentation of the world (made present to us artificially after the event) rooted in biases and skewed motives.

Every story that is featured in the news is the result of a human decision to accord it priority over others. "News is a choice, an extraction process, saying that one event is more meaningful than another event," writes Cole Campbell, the late editor of the *Virginian-Pilot*. "The very act of saying that means making judgments that are based on values and based on frames." Every cluster of stories presented on a given day, by a given news organization, is one of many possible combinations of narrative. The impression of the world that is created in the mind rests heavily on that recipe.

One of the more basic, and well-known, levels of news filtering is the tendency to report on negative events. Over time this has the impact of creating an impression that the world is constantly on the cusp of collapse. So much of what happens that is positive or neutral in value, the vast majority of events, slips through the dragnet and is thus omitted from the news "map." These include happenings which no journalist or news organization ever gets wind of—such as the many slow and unobtrusive trends that are at work in the world that aren't reported because they're not obviously dramatic.

Poverty, particularly extreme poverty, has been in decline around the world for decades. A study by Oxford economists Max Roser and Esteban Ortiz-Ospina determined that the number of people living in the most abject conditions of poverty went from 2 billion in 1990 to roughly 705 million in 2015. "On every day in the last 25 years," the authors write, "there could have been a newspaper headline reading, 'The number of people in extreme poverty fell by 137,000 since yesterday.'"

Harvard psychology professor and author Steven Pinker has championed the idea that violence in the world has declined both in the long-run and in the short-run (contrary to the impression made upon us by the news) and that, overall, we are the richest, most comfortable, best-fed, longest-lived people in history. We fail to appreciate how much progress the world has made because the news is usually so negative.

"News is about things that happen, not things that don't happen," writes Pinker, in his book *Enlightenment Now*. "We never see a journalist saying to the camera, 'I'm reporting live from a country where a war has not broken out'—or a city that has not been bombed, or a school that has not been shot up. As long as bad things have not vanished from the face of the earth, there will always be enough incidents to fill the news, especially when billions of smartphones turn most of the world's population into crime reporters and war correspondents."

This isn't to say that all is well in our world and that events reported in the news can't compound, spiral and end catastrophically for whole countries—or for the world. They obviously can. Clusters of extreme weather events might result in global food shortages in the future. Another worldwide pandemic, far deadlier than COVID-19, may break out. The Kashmir conflict, for instance, a continuing flash-point between India and Pakistan, may yet culminate in a nuclear war. There are many dire concerns in the world. But the point here is that a curated presentation of just the dire, day-in and day-out, is a distortion of a bigger picture that comprises both positive and negative developments—and a very wide spectrum of matters that fall in between.

It's not only the positive that gets underreported or left out—so do negative stories. Some of the worst fighting in the Syrian Civil War occurring at its climax in late 2019 and early 2020, which displaced around one million Syrians living in and around Idlib Province, went largely unmentioned in the western news media, partly because of its focus on the U.S. Democratic primaries, Donald Trump's impeachment hearings and the appearance of the first COVID-19 cases in Asia. This exclusion of otherwise newsworthy events—because they are crowded-out by more novel dramas—happens all of the time.

. That editorial neglect also occurs for other reasons. A story may be too obscure, too geographically remote, too difficult or expensive to produce, and/or contain too much necessary context. The words 'boring,' and 'unsexy' are subjective terms frequently spoken by news workers to disqualify the events that lie outside their list of checkboxes.

I offer this older example because it is illustrative in the extreme: between 1994 and 2003 the Democratic Republic of Congo (D.R.C.) in central Africa was embroiled in a war that eventually spread to nine nations and resulted in the deaths of around 5 million people. That conflict, sometimes dubbed 'Africa's First World War,' though no less brutish than any other war that gets featured in the news, was seldom mentioned in the Western media. A story from D.R.C., where violence continues to the present, might get the rarest mention on the slowest of news days today, but *only if* there's a tie-in with the West—if the story involves a major violent incident with the UN peace-keeping mission there, for example. If there's a large enough Ebola virus outbreak in the country, as sometimes happens, the news media will happily jump on it because of the unspoken but frightening (though highly unlikely) implication that the virus might one day spread to us.

Similarly, in the period between July 2017 and July 2018, the American network MSNBC gave no coverage to the U.S.-supported Saudi-led war against Yemen. That ongoing conflict, which fails to get the attention it deserves, created a humani-tarian crisis involving mass starvation coupled with an unprece-dented cholera epidemic that has infected over one million people. Yet in that same period MSNBC produced 455 segments about the Stormy Daniels scandal.[1]

As mainstream news gravitates ever more towards infotainment, with its pop culture and celebrity quotients, it isn't so much anymore that some news is excluded because there's not enough space or time to fit it, as much as what was once called "news" simply doesn't qualify as news at anymore.

EXAGGERATION

It is impossible to overrate the importance of context because nothing at all exists in isolation. It only ever exists in relation to other things. Quite simple building blocks of the world like time, space and motion, can only exist as relative to something else.

> – Iain McGilchrist, author, psychiatrist and literary scholar in an interview

THE NEWS IS CRAFTED to capture and hold our attention. It aspires to the highest standards of dramatic effect in order to pique our interest and have us coming back for more. Ratings, clicks, views, and subscriptions often hang tenuously on how shocking, sensational, outlandish, or seemingly unprecedented the events they highlight are. This desire to shock means that what is featured will often be exaggerated for effect, leaving us with a distorted view of how important and commonplace those events are.

Exaggeration in the news should not be seen as just an *act* of embellishment, but also an *effect* resulting from certain information—context—being withheld.

News is often reported in a vacuum devoid of its fuller context. The details of the core event dominate and takes centre stage, while other pertinent information is left by the wayside. This happens for a number of reasons. One is a lack of space, or time, to communicate the whole backstory. But another reason is that when enough context is conveyed it can completely change (sometimes in a positive sense) what the news means, how it's interpreted and how it impacts us psychologically. Yet doing this runs counter to *the message* news organizations want to communicate—and is therefore avoided. This is because *the ability to shock and fearmonger relies on the omission of qualifiers—additional information—that can mitigate those fears.* It wouldn't do to report, say, a great white shark attack on a surfer in Australia (a deeply disturbing event for those of us who love to swim in the ocean) while also stating that:

* more people die each year *separately* from lightning strikes, attacks by angry cows, and accidents with fireworks than from shark attacks;

* the attack happened in deeper water where big wave surfers tend to go, and is beyond where most bathers swim;

* the bottom of surfboards are visually appetizing to great whites who confuse them for traditional prey like seals;

* sharks don't deliberately prey upon people. The vast majority of them are not a danger to humans.

There is often more to consider with any given story. If the news is reported within a bigger picture of related facts or trends, it will usually seem less significant, shocking or worrying. It may even be disqualified as news. Hence focussing on just the core details of an incident—with minimal context—is emphasized in the delivery of hard news.

Exaggeration in the news takes two other primary forms:

1. Implicit exaggeration *by virtue of a story simply appearing in the news.*

2. Explicit exaggeration by those who report and/or produce the news.

Every story that appears in the news is exaggerated by the impact upon us of the medium itself. By being chosen, highlighted and focussed on, a story's importance is suddenly magnified in our minds—the story has made the news! Big online features and headlines on TV can alter our awareness in the same way that picking up any small object and holding it directly in front of our eyes can affect our visual perception, blocking much else out. Also, because hard news sticks to the facts of events, we are left to infer their significance or impact, sometimes wrongly. Our perception of risk, for example, can be rendered inaccurate as a result. News about a doctor treating parasites in a man who ate sushi, might imply that the now dreaded "sushi worm"—a new pestilence *du jour*—must infest all raw fish everywhere. Obsessive and alarmist coverage of foreign tourists getting killed in a militant bombing in Sinai, Egypt, as happened a few times between 2004 and 2006, sends an implicit and distorted message that the whole of Egypt and the Middle East are inherently dangerous. I've lost count now of how many people I've met in my life who've avoided travelling to places they've longed to visit because of memories of a violent incident once reported there.

In Canada, a country whose news coverage has traditionally been more tempered than that of its southern neighbour, sensationalism and exaggeration have become *de rigueur*. Stories once relevant and reported at only a local level such as disputes among the public, murders, criminal trials, and missing children are deliberately lifted from their narrower contexts and turned into stories of national importance in a bid to create outrage and draw maximum attention. CBC News Network, even though it is a publicly-funded broadcaster, pursues high TV ratings and online viewership and increasingly sells advertising—skewing its original mission and making it more susceptible to tabloidization. The network tries to compete within Canada against CNN and has adopted the latter's news model by focussing, when it can, on just a few big stories and live events over the course of the day—or week—at the expense of covering a greater variety of news items. That approach to coverage, though admittedly allowing for a more in-depth treatment of stories, leads invariably to the exaggeration of the importance—and thus distortion—of almost any given narrative.

In April of 2018, a bus carrying members of the Humboldt Broncos junior hockey team collided with a lorry in their home province of Saskatchewan, Canada, killing 16 people and injuring 13 others. The truck driver, who had failed to yield at a flashing stop sign at a highway intersection, was later charged with multiple counts of dangerous driving. Big Canadian news organizations, tapping the natural empathy most of us will feel about such a tragedy—not to mention the fanatical interest many Canadians have in hockey—went into overdrive with non-stop weeklong coverage of the event that was both melodramatic and voyeuristic.

Later, in 2019, the network again went into high gear, covering the impact statements of the victims' family members during the lorry driver's trial, which turned the event into a kind of public show trial against the accused who was predictably found guilty (what judge would rule against the outrage of an entire nation fired up by excessive news coverage?).

The bus accident was a tragic event for the families, friends and communities of those concerned. But as with many stories treated in such a way, its real significance was far out of proportion with the coverage it received. When a story is placed in front of you, and turned over endlessly, in an attempt to draw you in emotionally ever more deeply, a crucial piece of context is always lost, if not forgotten: that the said event is one of similar others in the world and often has no direct impact upon us to warrant the amount of coverage it receives—or energy we expend on it as an audience.

With news factories working in tandem like this to bring us the most shocking, tragic—and in some cases trivial—headlines, the impact on society is as marked as it is upon the individual. Our unmitigated consumption of hyperbole is transforming our culture, altering our shared values, perceptions and behavioural norms. By way of hypnotic suggestion, it prompts us to believe in, and to do things, we ordinarily wouldn't.

One of the best examples of this involves how the news media has changed the way we raise our children in North America. In the late 1980s and 1990s it became vogue for cable news and television programming to feature rare cases of missing children and child abductions. News stations and long form TV crime programs like *America's Most Wanted* inculcated the idea that kid-grabbing strangers lurk around every corner. Campaigns to raise awareness of this new issue quickly followed. Photos of missing kids began to appear on posters, milk cartons, baseball caps, grocery bags, and pizza boxes. "Norms changed, fears grew, and many parents came to believe that if they took their eyes off their children for an instant in any public venue, their kid might be snatched," write Jonathan Haidt and Greg Lukianoff in their book, *The Coddling of the American Mind.* "It no longer felt safe to let kids roam around their neighbourhoods unsupervised."

Yet while American society writhed in the throes of this faux crisis, the reality was, and still is, that child abduction and murder cases, though admittedly horrific, are among the rarest of crimes. The dangers are wildly exaggerated. Years of this fear-inducing sensationalism (nothing can command the attention and generate the empathy of a parent more than a terrible story involving someone else's child) has caused us to excessively shelter our offspring, preventing them from partaking in free-play and mild risk-taking, and which in turn has forged a generation of youth that is less resilient as they enter adulthood. Anxiety and depression among high school and university students is currently at an all-time high. This transformation, ironically, has occurred at a time when crime levels have generally plummeted. The enduring fear of kid-grabbing boogeymen, has helped turn North American society into an obsessive safety culture where parents can get into serious trouble if they are thought to be lax with monitoring their children.

As mentioned earlier, exaggeration also occurs as a more conscious, or habitual effort, by journalists, to make a story more enticing. This more explicit form involves the attempt to dress-up or sensationalize the news by crafting overly-dramatic headlines, using bombastic and fear-inducing language, or, in the case of television, by offering obsessive daylong, or multi-day, coverage. Writers in television newsrooms are often implored by their producers to "punch-up" or "jazz-up" the script to make a story more exciting (to disguise the fact that the occurrence may not be as dire as the news purports). The use of dramatic video footage to highlight a story is especially important in television and online. Video clips of protesters violently shouting, chanting, drum banging and scuffling with opponents or police will often be cherry-picked for a story about a political demonstration, even if the chaos only lasted briefly and the protest was mostly calm and peaceful. Nighttime images of volcanic eruptions and wildfires are preferred over daytime pictures for the obvious reason that they are more dazzling and menacing. Video footage of storms are sometimes sped-up to make them seem more dramatic than their mostly boring, drawn-out and intermittent fits and spurts would otherwise suggest. Even winter weather systems that, at worst, snarl urban traffic become headlines that are repeated *ad nauseum* throughout the day, creating an additional layer of stress and noise in our already overburdened lives.[1]

This type of deliberate amplification also takes place with much more serious stories that don't necessarily require embellishment. In January 2013, two U.S. Navy patrol boats with 10 crew on board were detained by Iranian forces when they strayed into that country's territorial waters in the Persian Gulf. When the event broke, a few major U.S. television news stations including Fox, MSNBC, and CNN described the soldiers as "hostages." Iran, well-remembered for its abduction and lengthy detention of Americans during the 1979 Islamic Revolution *also* later incarcerated British military personnel for weeks in hostage-like fashion during a similar maritime entanglement in 2007. The U.S. Navy crew, at that early stage of the incident, were detainees, as distinct from "hostages"—a term which suggests a very different political motive and circumstance, neither of which had been demonstrated.

That same day, while the American broadcasters obsessively speculated about all of the possible conflict scenarios that might arise from that "hostage" situation, other news media focussed on the positive political and diplomatic signals that indicated the crisis would quickly be resolved. The Associated Press headline that day, quoting in-the-know sources, read: "TWO U.S. NAVY BOATS IN IRANIAN CUSTODY BUT CREW WILL BE RETURNED 'PROMPTLY.'"

The sailors were released the next day.[2]

Even greater bluster was employed by the news media in October 2014 when a mentally disturbed Muslim-Canadian gunman shot and killed a soldier at the National War Memorial in Ottawa, Canada. After shooting the soldier, the attacker entered the nearby federal parliament building where a gun battle with security guards ensued, resulting in the assailant's death. Some U.S. media created hysteria around the admittedly dramatic event, implying something that it wasn't.

"ACT OF WAR" declared the print headline on the cover of *The New York Post*.

"TERRIFIED CAPITAL" and "TERROR IN CANADA – MULTIPLE SHOOTERS REPORTED IN ATTACK" were CNN's exaggerated and inaccurate online headlines.

The headline on the CBC News website that day was appropriately more prosaic by comparison:

"SOLDIER DIES AFTER PARLIAMENT HILL ATTACK, GUNMAN ALSO SHOT DEAD."

Exaggerated headlines are not confined to big political and international news. They infect, more commonly, less significant stories, especially the online clickbait-type pieces. An August 2017 *Toronto Star* online article about the proliferation of a pesky plant known as the "giant hogweed" greatly overplays its threat, making the risks it poses seem both immediate and omnipresent. "GIANT HOGWEED PLANT THAT CAN CAUSE BURNS AND BLINDNESS SPREADING IN CANADA," shouts the headline.

But the reality of the danger, we learn later, is much more nuanced. Yes, the plant can potentially cause third-degree burns if one's exposed skin comes into contact with it—*but only under specific circumstances*. Simply touching the plant isn't dangerous. Your skin must come into contact with the plant's sap, followed by lengthy exposure to the sun before the burning sensation and blistering takes place.

But we only learn of those caveats seven paragraphs into the article.

After also boldly declaring the risk to the public's eyesight in the headline, the writer thankfully lets us off the hook by quoting a research horticulturalist who tells us that blindness resulting from exposure to the giant hogweed would be very rare indeed. "You'd be hard-pressed to get it in your eye unless you were rolling around in the plant," the man says.

The article fails to precisely explain how quickly or widely the giant hogwood plant is "spreading" in Canada—or how authorities know. But by then it's already too late. We have by now seen the horror-film style headline and either out of fear for our children and ourselves—or simply for the morbid thrill— have clicked on it.

Hedging dangers and threats mentioned in a story with how little risk that thing actually poses in reality is seldom done by hard news journalists as it gets in the way of telling a good story.

WHO DOESN'T LOVE A GOOD STORY?
HOW WE ARE HARDWIRED FOR NARRATIVE

The rapid-fire, abbreviated format of television precludes complexities and nuance. Television is about good and evil, black and white, hero and villain. It makes us confuse induced emotions with knowledge.

– Chris Hedges, American journalist and academic

A VERY OLD Middle Eastern tale that has been recounted orally for centuries goes as follows:

There was once an old woman who lived by herself and who spent much of her time daydreaming on her balcony. One day an eagle landed on the railing beside her. The woman approached and grabbed the bird and held it aloft, examining it thoroughly. She had never seen an eagle before.

"Well, what an odd-looking pigeon you are," she said.

"I'm not a pigeon," the bird replied. "I'm an eagle!"

"Oh, don't be such a silly bird," the woman said chuckling. "I know a pigeon when I see one. You look a bit unkempt, but we'll fix things right."

She took the bird inside and began to make changes to its appearance. First, she clipped the bird's long talons. Then she straightened its bent beak. Finally, she combed-back the tuft of feathers on its head until it was flat.

"Fly away!" she said, flinging the bird from the balcony after grooming it. "Now you look more like you should!"

For millennia humans have told stories both to entertain and share knowledge. This first began with songs and oral traditions, followed later by the written word. Our survival as individuals and collectives often depended on our ability to assess and understand human power-relationships and conflicts which are well-conveyed in story form. The evolutionary need to share gossip—a mechanism for monitoring the moral behaviour of individuals within the group—also helped us become highly attuned to narrative. Thus, the human mind evolved to become a story processor. We are voracious consumers of narrative. Our brains are hardwired for it: bold and simple plot-lines that induce trance states during which we can absorb story patterns and thereby learn.

The news both reflects, and caters to, our sense of mythos and desire for universal narrative archetypes. This is why journalists often frame and refer to news items not as "news"—but as "stories." Furthermore, they are spun as dramas and plots involving villains, victims and heroes, which the media assigns to chime with whatever values that news organization—and parts of wider society—espouse. Rather than try to better understand events, highlight their complexity, and see the many sides of the issues underscoring them, news journalists encourage us to lose ourselves emotionally in the drama of characters; and perhaps to cheer and boo as if we were at a sports event. This is why Canadian audiences were so easily entranced by the Humboldt Broncos bus crash drama and why media organizations wouldn't just treat it as the terrible and unfortunate accident it was—and just move on from it.

"If a story can be arranged in this format, it will get media attention, often without a great deal of scrutiny as to who, exactly, the respective players are and by what criteria they were assigned to their roles," write David Murray, Joel Schwartz and S. Robert Lichter in *It Ain't Necessarily So: How the Media Remake Our Picture of Reality*. "A moral stage filled with heroes and villains, dangers and triumphs, greed versus disinterested sacrifice, alarms and escapes, dastardly cover-ups by the powerful, heroic unmaskings, and plucky underdogs successfully fighting city hall is embedded in the American psyche..."

With the huge success in the last decade of Netflix, HBO, Showtime, as well as many podcast series, the news has faced some stiff competition from other master storytelling platforms that weave the yarns we deeply crave. So triumphant have they been in capturing our attention—through the use of dramatic serials—that the news industry, especially in TV, has tried to emulate their soap-operatic formulas by drawing out coverage of news events for as long as possible to make them more serial-like. Anyone who regularly watches cable TV news will see more and more stories that play out consecutively for days and even weeks on end. By far the most extreme and obvious example of this is the interminable, years-long drama of Donald Trump's presidency which CNN, and other U.S. outlets, have featured day-in and day-out. The news industry was drawn to the Trump story as sharks are to blood. His early presidential ambitions met all the criteria of a potential dramatic serial (Trump himself was trained for years to perform on television). News executives correctly intuited that if Trump succeeded, his presidency would deliver a highly lucrative, entertaining and deeply interactive multi-platform reality series that would run for at least four years and lift news organizations out of their financial doldrums. It's a story in which real life came to imitate art: *The Sopranos* meets *The West Wing* meets *Law and Order* (we'll return to Trump and the news media later).

And then there was Harvey Weinstein. His 2018 sexual harassment and abuse scandal, which sparked the #MeToo movement, was another bit of serial manna from the news gods. The shocking and deplorable allegations made by so many women against one of the most powerful men in Hollywood—a reckoning that was far too long in the making—was an important story not just about a corrupt industry work culture but also about gender-relations across society.

But it was all the more sensational for a struggling news media who today thrive on stories about celebrities, scandals, sex, violence and crime. The villain, the heroes and the victims couldn't be more clearly delineated in this case. The story was milked over many weeks and months in all of its lurid details, hijacking news coverage and generating ripples of anger and resentment across society. News managers at CBC were naturally pleased by the ratings and clicks the Weinstein story generated, and, like other news organizations, worked to keep it in the headlines for as long as possible for partly that reason.

~

As entertaining as it may be, boiling down news events to the shenanigans of its *dramatis personae* in this manner obscures the less dramatic but important contextual complexities of those events that can help us better understand them—and ourselves. The problem is, we as an audience would much rather be told stories that are simple, basic and play to our pre-existing views of the world. Layers of complexity require too much extra mental energy to factor into a story. It also makes it difficult for us to take a hard position on an issue—which our tribal minds are predisposed to doing. We often *want* to express our anger. We want to condemn. We want to feel self-righteous. We want to connect and join with others in our denunciation. Ultimately, we want to feel moments of certainty in our largely uncertain lives. That's the fundamental purpose of dogma in human psychology.

There is no context that mitigates the severity of Weinstein's actions. Yet, in spite of his guilt, a fairly cut-and-dry case, and for all the weeks and months of media coverage there was little non-politically-driven discussion in the news about the deeper, wider, cultural issues underscoring the story. Why, for instance do we as a society place such a high value on celebrity, fame and attention—not to mention the enormous wealth that Hollywood dreams are made of—that a man like Weinstein can use it for leverage and some women would (and presumably did) consent to his monstrous advances? And just as importantly: what role does the media play—including the news media with its celebrity worship—in inculcating these values?

This template assigning heroes, victims and villains is applied to nearly any story that can accommodate it. That includes one of the most opaque and complex events that can unfold in our modern world: the economic crash. The global financial crisis of 2007–08, triggered, in part, by the subprime mortgage bubble in the U.S. was quickly shaped into a simple human drama. Front and centre were the villains who had undermined society: the bankers whose greed had caused the crisis and the governments (their enablers) that were bailing them out. Directing retribution against them was a movement made up of heroic grassroots activists who dubbed themselves 'Occupy Wall Street.' From their ad hoc protest camps in city streets across North America, they called for the bankers to be punished and for the system to be radically reordered. The victim was society at large and especially the common working person who must always bear the brunt of the robber barons' criminal sleights of hand.

But what the news didn't emphasize enough, because it distracts from the noise of the simpler human drama, is that responsibility for the global depression was shared by more than just the top bank executives. The stage was set for a collapse also because of actions and decisions by politicians, regulators, mortgage brokers, central bankers, retail creditors, and just as importantly, the general public, who took out loans they couldn't afford to pay back—and who maxed out their credit cards. Other economic trends and factors around the world also set the stage. It was, to borrow the term, "a perfect storm" of colluding factors. There are no single causes of events this large, so complex and far-reaching in their antecedents.

In the months after the 2003 invasion of Iraq, I travelled to Baghdad to work on a television documentary for the Arabic-language news station, Al Arabiya, which chronicled the war's immediate aftermath. While there I met an Iraqi man who told me that a local female artist and political cartoonist—one of the most accomplished in the Arab World—was killed in a 1993 U.S. airstrike. The bomb, which the Americans later said had gone astray, was meant to hit the headquarters of the Iraqi intelligence service. But the man I spoke to was convinced that the artist was deliberately assassinated by the White House because of her illustrations which mocked the U.S. administration. The idea that the woman may have simply been an unfortunate victim, caught in the crossfire of the war, was a possibility he couldn't accept.

Humans have a tendency to create their own explanations for events, after the fact, for which they don't have full or direct knowledge. Because we have a psychological bias for simplicity over complexity, the explanations we create tend to be simple, compelling, and concrete while downplaying the factors that would render different possible explanations. There is a term for this: *narrative fallacy*. The expression was coined by Nassim Nicholas Taleb in his book *The Black Swan* and was studied by the economic sciences Nobel Prize-winner Daniel Kahneman. It describes our desire to impose acceptable patterns upon complex events. All of us resort to this regularly, for example, when trying to interpret and explain the behaviours and motives of people around us including family, friends, and co-workers. On a larger scale, rather than recognizing and acknowledging the complexity of global events, we arrive at explanations based on our own mental models of the world. We manufacture causal relationships that make sense to us.

Creating narrative fallacies is the norm when it comes to explaining the concealed and complex world of politics—a realm which few people have little direct knowledge of, or experience with. Conspiracy theories, like the one related to me by the Iraqi, are narrative fallacies *par excellence*: simplistic explanations that try to impose order upon events whose causal relationships are more anarchical than they are linear and predictable.

Framing the news into stories with simple causation at their core is also a form of narrative fallacy. It is a tendency to order the world in terms of a fixed pattern. But as in the Middle Eastern story of the old woman determined to turn an eagle into a pigeon, shaping the news to fit a simpler story formula is a form of self-delusion that distorts reality. The world's goings-on are dizzyingly complex affair—a labyrinth of intertwined trajectories of cause and effect that, even when only partially glimpsed, contradict all comfortable notions of a single-cause universe.

Assigning blame is one of the most common forms of the narrative fallacy. The news media's use of the villain-victim-hero storytelling formula is central to this task. We live in a blame culture in which every error, failure, mistake, accident, or perceived and real injustice needs to be pinned squarely on someone else. This happens so much in part because our culture stigmatizes mistakes and failures. But it also stems from our need to bring order to disorder through simple explanations.

The problem with so readily shifting blame is that it prevents us from seeing more of what actually contributed to an event. "Blame undermines the information vital for meaningful adaptation," writes author Matthew Syed in his book, *Black Box Thinking*. "It obscures the complexity of our world, deluding us into thinking we understand our environment when we should be learning from it." Syed describes newspaper stories apportioning excessive blame as the "mass-printed by-products of the narrative fallacy."

After the rise of the Sunni militant group ISIS in Iraq and Syria, it became a western media pre-occupation to ask: *Who created ISIS? Who is to blame for ISIS?* After much bickering in the media a consensus emerged among many that the U.S. invasion and occupation of Iraq was alone to blame. Full stop. In the final months leading up to the 2016 presidential election, Donald Trump jumped on the bandwagon and began accusing Barack Obama and Hillary Clinton for "creating" ISIS. News organizations explored these facile avenues of blame, but few, if any, really went deep into the matter. The causal relationships that underpin this question are just too complex for news consumers—and even many journalists—to understand and appreciate. A blizzard of causes, going back decades, and whose origins lay primarily in the Middle East, helped create the ISIS phenomenon. The U.S. invasion and occupation of Iraq was one, albeit important, contributing factor. But in the bid to win ratings, clicks and subscriptions, sticking to the blame game— even if it's inaccurate, or incomplete, is easier than trying to explain that.

Our appreciation of reality suffers through the resulting distortion.

This tendency to determine single causation is so widespread that even when destructive natural disasters occur, blame immediately needs to be allotted—villains, victims and heroes are once again assigned and labelled.

The U.S. Federal Emergency Management Agency (FEMA) became the primary villain after Hurricane Katrina slammed into New Orleans in August 2005, causing widespread death, destruction and flooding. FEMA's bureaucratic ineptitude and mismanagement of the emergency response, as well as its general unpreparedness for the disaster, became the primary "cause" of the calamity which followed the storm. Through all of the finger pointing and accusations, no one mentioned that really *no one* could have been prepared for a storm of such a magnitude because to be truly prepared means having gone through such an event before, under the same—or similar—circumstances and having learnt from the process.[1] The political storm that was spawned in the hurricane's wake became a hot-button media topic for months and years to come.

"The notion that acts have agents, agents have intentions, and intentions therefore explain the acts seem to constitute the most compelling psychological template for journalists," write Murray, Schwartz and Lichter. "Unfortunately, this same logic is often applied not just to human actions but to events of the natural world as well. Thus, when something inexplicable happens in the world, be it a technological disaster or a natural catastrophe, journalists often seek the 'ulterior' forces that caused the event, their inquiry coming to rest upon a likely villain who had suspect intentions."

The hero-victim-villain formula sets an issue in stone from the outset. It prevents subtler ideas, information and perspectives from reaching an audience—and thus prevents a natural process of calibration towards a more accurate truth from occurring (the news media's approach to covering the coronavirus story is also an example of this[2]). Instead, all that matters are the protagonists with their right and wrong positions and the inculcation of emotion and 'moving the story forward' so that the audience will return for more. This approach may be entertaining at times, but it also qualifies as indoctrination—concealed within the Trojan horse of storytelling—that inevitably influences our thoughts and behaviours, and which feed back into the news.

'THE ARGUMENT CULTURE'

If you limit your view of a problem to choosing between two sides, you inevitably reject much that is true, and you narrow your field of vision to the limits of those two sides, making it unlikely you'll pull back, widen your field of vision, and discover the paradigm shift that will permit truly new understanding.

– Deborah Tannen, *The Argument Culture*

IN MARCH 2018, then former U.S. Vice President Joe Biden spoke at a rally against sexual assault and gender-based violence at the University of Miami. Taking aim at President Donald Trump's degrading comments about women, Biden said, "A guy who ended up becoming our national leader said, 'I can grab a woman anywhere and she likes it.' They asked me if I'd like to debate this gentleman, and I said 'no.' I said, 'If we were in high school, I'd take him behind the gym and beat the hell out of him.'"

When word of the unorthodox comments reached Trump, he fired back in his usual fashion, tweeting: "Crazy Joe Biden is trying to act like a tough guy. Actually, he is weak, both mentally and physically, and yet he threatens me, for the second time, with physical assault. He doesn't know me, but he would go down fast and hard, crying all the way. Don't threaten people Joe!"

The news media seized on this clash of political celebrities, framing it as an epic showdown to come and labelling it "Biden vs. Trump." In some cases the coverage came replete with sports-style tales of the tape including questions of who would win in a real fistfight—or in the 2020 election if they were to face each other.

News organizations relish covering stories about conflict. Disputes between humans have a primal attraction that instantly draws an audience, much in the way that a schoolyard fist-fight between rival bruisers magnetizes a crowd of morbidly fascinated children. This is why so much of what appears in the news media reflects some manner of dispute or conflict. To make coverage as exciting as possible the news often frames stories of discordant issues into deep conflicts reflecting seemingly irreconcilable differences. The fundamental intent is to mimic warfare: a human ritual whose purpose is not compromise, but the settling of differences through the vanquishing of one side by another. The news will frame people opposed on an issue, or in a story, as combatants who can either debate each other on TV, or be quoted in print or online at cross purposes. Journalists tend to focus on their differences rather than ideas that might constitute a solution.

On television—a more dramatic and hypnotic medium than print—contentious issues tend to take the form of staged fights between the guests. Other news shows will pit a single guest against a program's interviewer who assumes the role of a combatant taking the opposing view in the debate. CNN's once famous political talk-show program *Crossfire*,[1] the BBC News programme *HARDtalk*, and Al Jazeera English's *Head to Head* are among the better known versions of this format. All of them, incidentally, have names resonant of conflict.

The various so-called "Sunday talk shows" like *Fox News Sunday*, CBS's *Face the Nation* and NBC's *Meet the Press* have also sometimes used this approach of going deeper into contentious or controversial topics through curated debates. This style of brusquely hashing things out has its origins in the television talk show of Phil Donaghue and ABC News' *Nightline* with Ted Koppel, both of which were popular in the 1980s. These interviewers learned that they could create compelling and dramatic TV by bringing together guests with different opinions and letting them go at it like fighters in the ring. If interviewees, as they sometimes do, become emotional, lose their tempers, or in rarer cases, storm out of the interview, producers pat themselves on the back having achieved the crowning glory of creating "great TV."[2]

Deborah Tannen, an American author and professor of linguistics at Georgetown University in Washington, regards this tendency by the news media to view and portray the world in terms of warring dualities as part of what she calls an "argument culture." Tannen describes Western society, especially North America, as just such a culture; one conditioned by notions of dichotomy, dispute and ritualistic opposition and which glorifies conflict and aggression. Even the quickest glance at our media, politics and legal systems reveals them to be underscored by approaches that are black-and-white and deeply adversarial. Think: Super Bowl, filibusters, the lawsuit industry, high school and university debating teams, Republicans and Democrats, Jerry Springer, and, of course, the news. The battle metaphor is ubiquitous.

"At the heart of the argument culture," Tannen writes, "is our habit of seeing issues and ideas as absolute and irreconcilable principles continually at war." The argument culture in the news media doesn't just apply to the framing of topics, Tannen says, but extends to the bull-doggish attitude of journalists themselves who are constantly on the lookout for scandals, slip-ups, foibles, improprieties, and contradictions among those it reports on and holds to account—especially publicly-elected figures. This scandal-obsessed press is a direct legacy of the golden years of investigative journalism of the Vietnam and Watergate eras—huge victories of "unmasking" which the news media is continuously trying to replicate today, and which has now come to include celebrities and members of the general public as targets.

One of the more damaging manifestations of argument culture in the news is its ever-increasing habit of drawing its content from the battles that rage on social media, especially on Twitter. The reality distortion that occurs through this type of cheap and lazy journalism is amplified by the fact that Twitter is a virtual and disembodied forum that does not physically exist in any sense of the word. There are positive aspects to this technology, of course. But at its worst the platform is an anarchical tower of babble, where the loudest and most crafty opinion-mongers and dogmatists rise to the top of the broth through self-righteous monologues and pronunciations. Not unlike the news, Twitter distorts reality by caricaturing our world—but through a distillation of voices from an otherwise silent ocean of humanity. Twitter's unreliability is underscored by the fact that what is said there—and reacted to—often lacks context, is elicited reflexively in the heat of the moment (sometimes by bots and other agent provocateurs), and may not have been spoken if those discussions occurred face-to-face.

When controversies involving polarized people rage on social media—whether they be about verbal gaffes, claims of racism, gender issues or identity politics—and when the news media obsessively co-opts these into their coverage, journalists are giving disproportional representation to and amplifying these conflicts, creating the illusion that their points of contention reflect mass consensuses. They often do not. These spates are neither constantly flaring-up around us, nor do they involve us to the extent that the newsmongers would like us to think they do.

Stoking these conflicts also trains the wider public to view the world in black-and-white and either/or terms. By framing disputes between absolute, inviolable, positions (and avoiding shades of grey and complexity—which are considered anathema to drama), it creates the impression that other perspectives, or solutions, don't exist. We are left with the sense that only one, or the other, of two positions must prevail for the impasse to be broken. It also reinforces a false notion that dialogue between parties with differing ideas *must* take the form of deaf and blinkered debates between intransigents rather than an effort involving other parties to find a solution, or reach an acceptable compromise. This may be one of the greatest missed opportunities for conflict resolution in our times: the possibility of using media forums to *mediate* between sides and seed contentious issues with their possible solutions.[3]

Filtering issues through the lens of left versus right—the most readily available, convenient and seemingly universal duality for pitting opponents against one another—conditions the masses to viewing life through that very same lens. This tendency to place everyone and everything into one camp, or the other, inevitably means that people who don't entirely fit into either must nonetheless be labelled as one or the other—rendering their unique ideas and subtleties of opinion void. The idea that somebody must be one thing or the other, 'with us or against us,' is a core mental frame of tribalists whose conflict-prone perception-set has caused so much persecution and suffering throughout history. Making news about two sides with contradictory claims feeds the argument culture, stokes binary thinking, promotes social media bickering and contributes to the general polarization of society that we are currently witnessing. It also encourages violent conflict and civil unrest. There can be no deeper understanding or solutions-based new thinking for the problems we face because competing claims exhaust our attention and then cancel each other out.

THE OBJECTIVITY MYTH

To see 'both sides' of a problem is the surest way to prevent its complete solution. Because there are always more than two sides.

– Idries Shah, *Reflections*

It's what Nick Davies, the award-winning British journalist, writer and filmmaker calls the "great blockbuster myth of modern journalism": that the news media reports, or strives to report, "objective" truth. The idea that journalists must always cover "both sides" of a story equally and with cool detachment is deeply embedded in our culture. Journalists are indoctrinated with this idea when they are trained and are later frequently reminded of it by way of clichéd mantras from their peers and superiors in the newsroom. "We need to give equal weight to the opposing viewpoint," the saying goes, as if a holistic pursuit of truth were always made up of just two halves that are in every way always equal. This simplistic understanding of reality means the news is yet again shaped to meet artificial criteria. The result is another veil of distortion: a whitewash of the story arrived at through the stripping away of perspective.

The attempt to find "balance" by telling "both sides" of a story has nothing to do with objectivity and everything to do with taking a stance of *neutrality*. This is a deteriorated understanding of what real objectivity is: a position vis-à-vis reality drawing on *numerous* perspectives that approach a whole. The reflex to assume a neutral stance in journalism likely originated long ago as a safeguard to prevent media members and news organizations from pushing their own agendas—whether collective or individual. Our democratic and egalitarian culture that preaches fairness and even-handedness also reinforces this tendency to seek impartiality. As does the dichotomy of the argument culture. Fear by journalists and news organizations of being wrong helps to etch that rule into stone.

Appearing neutral in reporting means playing it safe. Davies calls it a "coward's compromise aimed at dispatching quick copy with which no one will quarrel." It also means cancelling out, or negating certain positions and arguments by giving equal value to their opposites.

I saw excessive forms of this while working as a writer at CBC News Network, especially when it came to some of its reporting on issues and events related to the Israel-Palestine conflict. Fear of a public backlash, particularly from pro-Israel pressure groups and Arab activists who intensely scrutinize the content of news organizations, led at times to a neurotic hair-splitting process in the newsroom in which many producers redacted the language in finished copy to an extent that ultimately drained the stories—involving violence from one or both sides—of much clarity and meaning.

When looked at closely we see that most controversial stories are made-up of a dizzying matrix of causes, contradictory truths and rights and wrongs. Approaching *real* objectivity in the news, and in everyday life, means cultivating a holistic, flexible and nimble approach to perceiving the world that is an amalgam of interwoven perspectives and contexts. This is exceedingly difficult, if not impossible, to do in hard news journalism because of the need for brevity, and also because some stories demand a point-of-view approach for the purposes of story-telling; the hero-villain-victim formula demands it. We are furthermore all influenced by biases, emotions and culturally conditioned beliefs. Because of this, journalists either produce skewed versions of news that favour one protagonist over another (to understand a news organization's editorial bias, look to its heroes and villains), or they manufacture artificially "balanced" stories giving equal weight to protagonist claims that end up being blandly even-keel and incomplete.

This is why objectivity in the real sense does not exist in journalism whether by intent, or in deed. It's also why *all* news media, even those with the best practices and methods, will always distort the world to some extent.

IT'S ALL JOURNALESE TO ME

Language can be very adept at hiding the truth.
   - Dan Brown, *The Lost Symbol*

IN HARD NEWS, the need to keep writing brief, to adhere to facts and to appear "objective" (read: neutral) has led to a form of language particular to the craft sometimes called "newspeak" or "journalese." It is a shorthand-style of writing composed of clichés and convenient turns of phrase, that feels a bit like its own language. Because there is neither sufficient space in print and online, nor time in TV news and radio broadcasts, to explain stories in all of their context, the writing must cut corners and be highly compressed. Euphemisms take over. The result is a stilted language rendered somewhat tasteless and colourless and which more often than not detaches us from the story.

We've become so conditioned to this use of language that it barely registers as odd anymore. Journalese recreates a world in which: 'clashes erupt,' hurricanes 'leave people dead,' people 'face' probes, economies are 'hit' by recessions and events are 'widely seen' in various ways. It is a realm inhabited by cookie-cutter archetypes such as fugitive financiers, slain civil rights leaders, grieving widows, embattled politicians, troubled youth, uncertain futures, deepening political crises, restive populations, and rogue states.

The fundamental problem with this approach to writing is that it further reduces a highly complex, living and ever-changing reality to the most static caricatures and snapshots, thereby passing it through yet another prism of distortion. Words hold different meanings and values to different people that change according to context. Language can never properly capture and do justice to reality and human experience—at best it creates a *re*-presentation of that which is described. Even long-form journalism, which is aeons ahead of hard news in its ability to communicate nuance, can still only offer a thin slice of its subjects and stories. The dissonance between the real thing and its caricature generated by hamstrung news workers inevitably translates into inaccuracy and falsehood.

Journalese also creates unintended meanings and implications. Among the more common and humorous are the distortions of meaning that sometimes occur in headlines because of their compressed, abbreviated and truncated natures. The urgency and speed at which headlines are churned out can also prevent their authors from seeing the ambiguity and double-meanings that might be found in them. Here are a few documented examples from some newspapers over the years:

—POLICE SQUAD HELPS DOG BITE VICTIM

—EIGHTH ARMY PUSH BOTTLES UP GERMANS

—CHILD TEACHING EXPERT TO SPEAK

—WOMAN BETTER AFTER BEING THROWN FROM HIGH RISE.

—SOLAR SYSTEM EXPECTED TO BE BACK IN OPERATION

—DRUNK GETS NINE MONTHS IN VIOLIN CASE

Similar misunderstandings can present in journalistic copy across all media. For instance, during the COVID-19 pandemic, many publications referred to the virus as the "deadly coronavirus." Although SARS-CoV-2 has killed more people in proportion to the normal seasonal flu, the vast majority of those infected survived (and far more than we can perceive because their stories are never featured in the news). Calling it "deadly" all the time implies an inevitability about its lethality and works to sensationalize the story and frighten the public more than it already is. Though car traffic kills scores of people every year by way of accidents, we don't refer to regular commuter car activity as "deadly traffic." The same applies to swimming pools, oceans, and snow.

When reporting on the Syrian civil war, the news media have often used the term "moderate opposition" to denote the ragtag groups of armed and violent Sunni militias fighting the Assad regime who haven't—at least in the mind of most journalists—attained the highest bar of religious fanaticism and viciousness set by groups such as ISIS or what was formerly called the al-Nusra Front. Yet who would describe and label any armed rebel group fighting to overthrow a government as "moderate"? The fact that many of those roving gangs were motivated by religious doctrine, held deeply conservative beliefs and were supported by some Islamist governments, also belies their moderate disposition. Here language fails: the news is trying to convey that because these groups were also supported by the West (i.e. – us) and were not as fanatical as ISIS and their apocalyptically-minded confreres, they must therefore be reasonable and open-minded. The journalese shorthand "moderate," chosen to convey that, fails to jibe with reality.

Similarly, how many times in the past have we heard the expressions "peace process," "peace talks," or "unity talks" used to describe what are at best reluctant, but more often forced meetings between unequal political rivals who haven't come near approaching the prerequisite consensus that is the basis of reaching a political compromise in good faith? Political negotiations in Israel-Palestine, Iraq, Syria, and Yemen have been described using this overly-optimistic terminology. Yet the majority of those meetings and processes are dead-end cul-de-sacs—sideshows of conflict, often organized by outside powers and agencies that are agreed-to by the participants for the purposes of optics and attention-exchange. Such language misconstrues the intent and the likelihood of success of those meetings. In the generalizing mind of the news professional, the fact that rivals are meeting at all—though not entirely meaningless—indicates that peace and agreement are somehow seriously on the cards.

Again, these assumptions riddle the news. As the authors of *The Arabist*, a blog about Middle East politics, write: "It doesn't take much to see a 'national unity government' in Baghdad instead of a profoundly unbalanced and dysfunctional cabinet; we say 'Iraqi army' for what in reality is a worn-down collection of abused and often corrupt men who fled as the Islamic State advanced and left most of the fighting to Shia militias. We posit 'ceasefires' in Syria to refer to surrenders under the regime's bombardment, siege and starvation..."

When these expressions are repeated endlessly, they become established in our everyday language and consciousness. They create false knowledge of what is going on in the world. Reality is misrepresented.

COLOURED BY NUMBERS

People are always wondering why the piling of fact on fact, from all sorts of sources, carried on by some researchers, yields so little. I can only quote the saying: 'You can never find out the time in a clock shop.'
  – Idries Shah, *Observations*

IN 2012, a CBC News reporter, Kelly Crowe, wrote an article for the CBC's online health blog entitled "It's news, but is it true?" Her piece looked at the problems involved with reporting the findings of scientific and medical studies in the news. She cited a number of academics who suggest that much coverage of scientific studies by newspapers is not only flawed, but involves research that ends up being refuted or attenuated over time.

Journalists love to report studies that are at the "initial findings" stages—research that claims to be the first time anyone has discovered a thing—because there is newsworthiness in their novelty. But "first ever" discoveries are also extremely vulnerable to becoming undermined by subsequent research. When that happens, the news media often don't go back and inform their audiences about the change—assuming they even hear about it. "There is increasing concern that in modern research, false findings may be the majority or even the vast majority of published research claims," says one epidemiologist that Crowe quotes. The CBC reporter goes on to suggest that journalists, though blameworthy for this tendency, are aided and abetted by the scientists whose studies they cite. She writes that the "conclusions" sections in scientific abstracts can sometimes be spun or overstated in an attempt to garner attention from prestigious academic journals and media who uncritically take their bait. Crowe ends her piece by stressing that there is an incompatibility between the purposes and processes of news and science. "Science 'evolves,' but news 'happens,'" she writes. "As reporters, we want to be able to tell you the 5 Ws, the Who, What, Where, When and Why of the story, with absolute certainty, even though in science it's almost impossible to be eternally certain about anything."

Crowe's blog post is a rare and commendable example of dissenting journalism that critiques the work of her colleagues and the industry that employs her. Anyone who pays even the slightest attention to the news knows that scientific study stories can feature very prominently. There have been so many contradictory claims reported by journalists with great enthusiasm about the health benefits—or lack thereof—of things like coffee, red wine, dark chocolate and red meat, that it's nearly impossible to say with any certainty what the truth actually is. Studies about what may, or may not be, cancer-causing is another unending news obsession because, even if that study can only demonstrate a slight correlation, it grabs people's attention instantly. These type of stories are traditional pillars of the news cycle partly because audiences tend to be older, and thus more health and mortality conscious, so the news is magnified in their own minds as it caters to their hopes and fears.[1] When journalists repeatedly feature "new research" that seems to reverse a previous finding on the same question, news organizations are actually feeding the argument culture. It is one side countering the other in what they frame as a debate. But in doing so, they actually sow greater confusion within society.

Few stories are trickier, more questionable and loaded with hard-to-know context than those involving scientific studies and statistics. The factors at play in these stories makeup another subset of prisms and filters that can skew journalism—and reality. Here are a few:

* It is fairly well-established that some scientific and health studies are funded by special interests like the pharmaceutical or other arms of the health industry and are therefore compromised by bias.

* The news media tends to value studies published in the more prestigious scientific journals (*Nature, Science, Lancet, Journal of the American Medical Association*) over those studies that are equally or more compelling, but are published in smaller, lesser known publications.

* The news media has little time, space, ability and incentive, to qualify the findings of scientific studies in their news reports, instead preferring to simplify what their authors conclude. That simplification is aided and abetted by scientific press releases about those studies that spread hype about initial findings.

* Research journals don't tend to publish studies that show null observations—where nothing happened. And those studies therefore never make the news even though proving that 'something isn't there' is extremely important in the overall advancement of knowledge.

* When the press reports statistical increases or decreases in certain phenomena—such as types of crimes, diseases or deaths —they tend to be increases or decreases of *reports* of those things. They are not usually reflective of how often those events occur in totality (both reported and unreported).

* Individual studies that show a link between one thing and another are far less compelling and reliable as evidence (because they may be flukes or anomalies) than what are called "meta-reviews," which are a group of similar studies in aggregate. But the latter tend to be less publicized and harder to understand.

* Much research, especially dietary studies, tend to involve too many variables for their conclusions to be taken at face value. For example, studies that try to ascertain the nutritional value of organic versus nonorganic produce are problematic because there are so many additional farming conditions and practices that can impact the quality and nutritional value of produce, whether it is organic or not.

One serious, recurring issue is that the correlation a study draws between phenomena is not necessarily causal in the way the study might imply. In other words: what scientists (and journalists) might assume to be the cause of something may in fact be due to another variable which presents alongside it, but which is less obvious.

For instance, there have been studies that have linked low levels of vitamin D with Alzheimer's disease. That is the extent of the finding. But the media, and by extension the general public, including some in the medical profession, have embraced the notion that that relation is causal: low vitamin D can cause Alzheimer's. Seems reasonable. But not only does this view ignore the scores of other factors that determine if a person is afflicted with the illness, it also overlooks the possible *reverse causation* demonstrated in the study. It could very well be that Alzheimer's patients tend to show vitamin D deficiency *because of their condition*. People suffering from that affliction are on the whole less mobile, less able to get about, and as a result stay indoors more often and get less sunshine.

Similarly, a body of research that has been building for years, suggests that people who live together prior to getting married are more likely to get divorced than those who don't. But as Oliver Burkeman, a former *Guardian* columnist writes: "Part of the reason for the discrepancy isn't about cohabitation, but the kind of people we already are when we decide whether to cohabit. If you're strictly religious, you'll be much less likely to move in before marriage, and less likely to split up if things don't go well. Whereas if you're the kind of convention-flouter willing to scandalise elderly family members by cohabiting, you'll surely also be more willing to contemplate divorce."

Non-scientific laypeople—including busy, time-strapped journalists sifting for headlines—have little idea how complex and technical these health risk studies are. Few people understand that epidemiology, the science of looking for risk factors by comparing populations, is never able to establish causation beyond a shadow of a doubt. All the studies can demonstrate is 'association,' a term that many of us tend to confuse with causation. "We mistake correlation for causation, and coincidence for conviction," write Murray, Schwartz and Lichter. "Hence we are continually fooled into thinking that we know something when we really don't. When all goes well in an epidemiological study, one finds an association between two things. No more, no less."

The need to probe studies more deeply and show how they can be read in alternative ways to draw radically different conclusions from the same data goes against the prime directive of news culture: the need to generate drama. The qualifications, caveats, and uncertainties that are inherent in scientific research are sometimes ignored by news journalists because those factors undermine the sense of certainty and simplicity that makes news so clear-cut and emotion-inducing.

"What it means in the real world," Crowe tells us in her CBC piece, "is that although science shows up in the headlines in black and white, it should instead appear in the infinite shades of grey that more accurately reflect the inherent uncertainty."

A 2017 article in *Vox* does just that. Likely inspired by Crowe's earlier blog post, the *Vox* piece reported that *half* of studies we read about in newspapers are later discovered to be inaccurate. *Vox* cites a follow-up study to the one mentioned by Crowe, conducted by the same author, but which was more thoroughly researched. The researcher concluded again, but with greater certainty, that newspaper journalists tend to preferentially report on first discovery-type initial findings in biomedical studies—and that they often don't inform readers when those studies are overturned.[2] At the end of the piece, however, the *Vox* writer urges caution by reminding the reader that the study only focussed on newspapers—and that the findings don't necessarily extend to other media. *Vox* also includes a quote from an email from the study's lead author which reads, "Our result only refers to a small sample of the scientific research. Also, we cannot extrapolate these results to other domains such as physics and chemistry."

FROM PR TO PROPAGANDA
THE ORIGINAL FAKE NEWS

THE ISSUE OF "FAKE NEWS" is all the rage these days. But few of us know that there have always been various shades of what we might call "fake news" running through the mainstream media—long before Putin's Russia, and others, got into the digital disinformation game.

Hard news is saturated with propagandistic information stemming from public relations efforts which are dressed-up as news stories. Not only do most of the public not realize this, but neither do many journalists, who are too busy and desperate for new content to spot it—or even care. The culprits are any organization with an agenda and an effective PR machine to push it: from think-tanks, to large corporations, to academic institutions and governments. Their "stories" span the spectrum of falsehood: from biased self-promotion to blinkered political opinion to complete fabrication.

The weapons of mass destruction (WMD) imbroglio in the lead-up to the 2003 Iraq War and the Y2K millennial bug scare are among the biggest and best-known examples of PR-driven fake news stories in the last two decades. But there are many less dramatic examples. Lots of product announcements, political punditry, travel stories, medical and pharmaceutical news, reports on technological breakthroughs and stories about the arts—just to name a few—carry the imprint of PR. Taken together that's a fair chunk of the news we consume.

PR-inspired stories can unduly influence the public, take up limited writing and broadcast space, and render the news as trivial. As Nick Davies, the author of *Flat Earth News* writes, "PR material is clearly inherently unreliable as a source of truth, simply because it is designed to serve an interest."

While at CBC News Network, I saw lots of this kind of PR material being churned into news content. The release of new Apple iPhones and iPads, for instance, has hijacked the organization's headlines over the years. In 2018, former Kiss band-member Gene Simmons was interviewed at the station (in his dark sunglasses) about his involvement in the medicinal cannabis company Invictus. It was a plug for his pot business, seemingly in return for lending his celebrity presence to the show. A year earlier, in 2017, the station went big with a story in the morning hours about Oprah Winfrey launching her own food brand. The opening lines of the news presenter's on-camera intro, before introducing the guest who spoke for several minutes on the "story," gives some indication as to the topic's gravitas:

> "Oprah Winfrey is known for bringing new life into everything she endorses. And now, Kraft Heinz is hoping she can work some of her magic with them. The entrepreneur announced today she will be teaming up with the company to launch her own food brand..."

The triviality of a story like this is one issue. Another is that it turns serious journalists and their organizations into lackeys for companies. Featuring products in this way also does a disservice to consumers as it promotes the claims made by their makers with little or no scrutiny. This isn't to say that lighter stories, retail and consumer news, shouldn't be featured. But they should be deemed to be in the public's interest to know (CBC's show 'Marketplace' does a good job of this at times, operating as a watch-dog for the consumer by investigating claims of falsehood in the retail and service sectors).

When news outfits run content like the Oprah PR item they are generally capitalizing on the "celebrity factor" for ratings and clicks. Uptake of PR content results in a commercial quid pro quo: an unspoken arrangement whereby the content provider says, "By helping sell our product (or message), you'll get content for your audience *and* a boost for your media brand if that content is popular." When a story's journalistic merit is so readily relegated to these sorts of considerations, journalism is undermined.

This is notably the case with political PR too.

Before the COVID-19 pandemic, Canadian Prime Minister Justin Trudeau, who is known for his optics and image-management artifice, had a penchant for pulling PR stunts directed at the corporate news media. He and his handlers have often staged "events" in which he appears spontaneously in public settings. Those "unexpected" sightings happened to be caught on camera and video, usually by his personal photographer who was looming somewhere in the background. Trudeau has appeared shirtless (as Vladimir Putin is known to do) for a jog in Toronto, has gone kayaking on waterways near residential areas to speak with locals, and has popped-up peek-a-boo style virtually anywhere in public to take a selfie with groups of people. During Trudeau's honeymoon period with the news media in the first two years after his 2015 election win, CBC News, along with many other big media organizations—some of them international—took the raw celebrity click-bait material he offered, running them as light news items. Like with Oprah's product placement it's always a popular story because it's fun and people love celebrities. It also happens to be good for Trudeau—which is why he goes out of his way, taking time out of his important Prime Ministerial duties, to do it.

But it's not news. It also wrongly skews our image of him and draws our attention away from what he is doing—or not doing—as a leader.

All of this may not be "fake news" in the sense that it is untrue or didn't happen, but it is certainly fake news in the sense that it is a fabricated pseudo-event and story *masquerading as real news*.

But propaganda can also be much more heinous and involve people with murkier motives than the bubbly PR and publicity professionals hired to create hype and influence opinions about private sector products and services. The world's intelligence services have always had an influence on what appears—or doesn't appear—in the news media. There is a long and documented history of espionage organizations, starting in earnest during the Cold War, using journalists to not just collect information but to sow confusion and disinformation using the media. In the lead-up to the Arab-Israeli Yom Kippur War fought in 1973, Egyptian intelligence planted stories in newspapers meant to disguise the fact that the country's military were massing forces on its side of the Suez Canal in preparation for a surprise attack. A few years later, and closer to home, U.S. congressional probes of intelligence abuses in the mid-1970s as well as related media investigations discovered that the CIA had hundreds of media assets worldwide that it had used regularly for decades, including in many mainstream news organizations. CIA officials later told an academic researcher that they planted 70 to 80 stories a day in the foreign news media in the late 1980s. Many Cold War intelligence memoirs written by retired professional spies from both sides of the Iron Curtain refer to such covert efforts at inserting fake stories in the press.

Most aggressive and able-bodied intelligence services have journalists on their payrolls, and there is no reason to assume that the same covert propaganda practices don't continue in the mass media to this day. In fact, a high-level Chinese intelligence operative who defected to Australia in 2019 revealed that media manipulation continued to be a pillar of its covert propaganda operations. An anonymous intelligence official quoted in a *Washington Post* article a few years earlier about political espionage and disinformation quipped, "It's regular intelligence procedure to try and influence a country's policies through the press."

The reason the Russian government has been so persistent with its fake news and digital subversion efforts on social media is because disinformation (*dezinformatsiya* in the jargon of Russian espionage) was always a specialty of the its main spy service, formerly known as the KGB; part of a larger Soviet intelligence effort known as "active measures," which was designed to sow chaos and confusion in the West. In one campaign, known as "Operation Denver," the KGB, along with the East German Stasi, spread false scientific research and news reports to suggest that HIV did not originate from primates in Africa but, was instead, fabricated by the U.S. Army. A 1987 Associated Press story about that theory was picked up by a TV producer and ran soon afterwards on the CBS Evening News. The story quickly spread around the world and continues to have numerous proponents.

It is also not well-known that the iconic footage showing Iraqi citizens cheering and rallying around the toppling of Saddam Hussein's statue in Fardos Square in Baghdad at the start of the 2003 Gulf War was a U.S.-staged ploy. "To this day, American television airs the footage as if it were a spontaneous act of jubilant Iraqis," writes former CNN journalist Jeff Cohen in his book *Cable News Confidential*. "A U.S. Army study has revealed that it was the work of U.S. Marines backed by army psychological warfare operatives, who rounded up Iraqi civilians to cheer. The idea to bring down the statue came from a U.S. Marine colonel."

Similarly, Nick Davies in *Flat Earth News* tells us that the rise to prominence of the late Jordanian Al Qaeda leader, Abu Mussab al-Zarqawi, stemmed from a false propaganda effort of the Jordanian and U.S. governments. According to Davies, Washington and Amman wanted to further justify their own anti-terror operations in the post-9/11 period by excessively demonizing and magnifying the threat posed by other al-Qaeda personalities, including Zarqawi, who, originally was a relatively inconsequential jihadist. The exaggerated tales woven about him found their way into the world's media, where they became further sensationalized and spread, creating a cult of personality around the man throughout the Muslim world—and thus a kind of self-fulfilling prophecy. The formerly minor extremist, who no doubt must have been surprised by his sudden and inexplicable rise to militant stardom, saw a surge of overnight support and was driven to acts of violence that took many lives.

Falsehood in the news manifests more widely than is recognized or understood. As demonstrated so far in this work it comprises many things, both fringe and mainstream. Both old and new. Both intended and unintended. And it also stems from the way journalists do their jobs.

PART II

THE NEWS FACTORY

When human atoms are knit into an organization in which they are used, not in their full right as responsible human beings, but as cogs and levers and rods, it matters little that their raw material is flesh and blood. What is used as an element in a machine, is in fact an element in the machine.

– Norbert Wiener, *The Human Use of Human Beings*

THE MAN BEHIND THE CURTAIN

It is not always a question of the Emperor having no clothes on. Sometimes it is, 'Is that an Emperor at all?'
— Idries Shah, *Reflections*

FOR MANY PEOPLE the news commands authority, because, like any professional class, journalists are naturally considered to be masters in their craft. This authority is bolstered by appearance-engineering and posturing. It derives from the squeaky-clean and highly packaged presentation and delivery of the news. Print and online publications feature attractive design and attention-grabbing headlines that ooze credibility. In the growingly archaic realm of cable television, news broadcasts are led by confident-looking and often attractive and immaculately groomed hosts whose delivery is just as flawless. Their unscripted humour and off-the-cuff remarks are meant to remind you (and perhaps themselves) of their humanity, and add to their likability. Their unseen counterparts, radio news announcers, speak in resonant hypnotic tones and rhythms. It's hard to blame anyone for consciously, or unconsciously, regarding those in the corporate news media as omniscient authority figures. Their firm and unshakable pronouncements can sound much like how we imagine a voice of God.

But appearances can be deceiving. The delivery is only the visible tip of a much larger iceberg that is the whole news production cycle. And though news journalism can be very good in quality, exceptional even, it is often riddled with problems, issues and hiccups behind-the-scenes that are invisible to the viewer. Just as the questing characters in the film *The Wizard of Oz* see the wizard at first only as an awe-inspiring image projected onto a wall (before the real and uninspiring "wizard" is found behind a curtain), the public see the whole news operation as just the final product—and not what goes into producing it. That reality is an anarchical and chaotic war room of rushed and often improvisational work.

Media newsrooms have a distinct and industry-specific work culture with certain modi operandi, work conditions, habits, and business considerations, which, like the other factors previously mentioned, further shape the product that they produce and which society consumes with few questions. Each newsroom, and each journalistic medium, has a different version of these dynamics. The main point is that these processes work as a prism to further reduce and warp the reality that is being depicted.

Just as we have a right to know how and under what conditions other products we consume are made—such as the food we eat—news consumers should be able to know what goes into "making" the news. I will strive here to share a few of my experiences, observations and lessons culled not just from working in a few television newsrooms over the years—but as a lifelong consumer of news of all mediums.

Caveat emptor.

'CHURNALISM'

We currently lead lives based on the assumption that anything that may be speeded up, should be. Accelerated is best, will lead to an enhancement of efficiency. This approach rests on a failure to understand that some things need to be done slowly.
    – Chris Ross, *Tunnel Visions*

Haste is from the Devil.
    – Arab proverb

Working as a news journalist means living life in the fast lane. Tight deadlines, sometimes many tight deadlines over the course of a day, serve a spurious assumption: that if you are not the first person to report something, then your audience will get it from another source.[1] Hence churning stories out as quickly as possible is still paramount in the news business. Every other consideration, including even the need for accuracy, becomes secondary when stories break. When advertising and TV cable subscription revenues used to flow like rivers of honey and there were enough newsroom staff to shoulder the heavy burdens, producing news was still a demanding and high-pressure rush to market. Today, evaporated budgets and mass layoffs means that some journalists do the equivalent of what was once the work of two or three colleagues just to keep the operation viable and afloat.

Ask anyone working in the most demanding news environments today—there is no time to think and do a proper job. Diligent copy editing is out the window. Thorough fact-checking, beyond a quick look-over, has become a long-abandoned craft. Reporters who once specialized in one medium, or beat, are now required to cover anything and everything. They also have to file their stories for multiple platforms. If you can take on a podcast series for what you're already getting paid, your job security might benefit a little bit more.

That frenetic work reality has spawned a term for the hard news business: "churnalism." Newsrooms have become factories, churning out product, often mindlessly and far too quickly, in a strange throwback to the industrial revolution. "A sausage factory" was how one former national news presenter described the newsroom to me before leaving to work at a local station in another Canadian province, where he hoped the pace would be less manic (work from home routines during COVID-19 have slowed matters down a smidgen, but the general pressure-cooker atmosphere still presides).

In cable television news, whether as a producer or writer, you arrive at your job before your particular show is about to go to air. You often have limited knowledge of and control over what stories will be featured that day. As a result, you will sometimes inevitably have no background information about the topics and events that are usually just coming to light and unfolding somewhere else, sometimes very far away. Stories can be dauntingly complex, confusing, highly nuanced or subject to labyrinths of legalese. But when you arrive, you immediately begin to work on not just one, but a handful of those stories, and are pressed, at the sound of a starting gun, to churn them out and prepare them in succession. New, breaking stories often suddenly appear that must also be quickly assembled.

It is impossible to provide a detailed picture of the full operation, but here's a brief description of working conditions in the milieu of television.

Ever-changing teams of people working together are not just spread out across the newsroom, but also across the country and sometimes around the world, involving producers, writers, story editors, video editors, reporters, control room technicians, field producers, interviewees at their homes or offices, managers, executives, lawyers, presenters, graphics people, technical resources people—and others. Interdependence underscores the entire operation: everyone needs help from everyone else to get their own job done. But every player is overloaded and is juggling too much of what they already have to do for themselves. No one has the complete picture of what is happening. Every person is waiting to receive at least one bit of information from someone else. The reporter you are working with—who is sometimes an underpaid freelance journalist appearing on Skype from their basement apartment—usually knows little more than what you know from the wires or web about a story. Script editors, who are under even more pressure than writers, only have time to do superficial fact-checking.

The pace is frenetic. Vectors of miscommunication are the rule, not the exception. Gaps in information are legion. Because of overloaded brains people forget to say, or do things, in spades. Problems and issues that can, and do, appear down the road are not anticipated. Meanwhile, ever-shortening deadlines hang over everyone like guillotines. People vanish from their desks or stations at the most inopportune moments to grab a bite, take a personal call or go to the bathroom. Emails are missed or not read. Ringing phones are not picked up. Computers freeze and video editing programs crash at the most inopportune times. Tempers flare. People succumb to anxiety, rages and meltdowns.

Meanwhile the clock continues to tick on, indifferent to all of it. The show plans change on the smallest whims or worries— often by diktat from overly-ambitious, blinkered producers who play unquestioningly by the formulaic rulebook. Information needs to be constantly updated or corrected. New news, sometimes of an unfamiliar nature, appears suddenly. Older stories are axed and shuffled off into the trash-bin vortex. All of this happens not just before a show goes to air, but also when it is *already* on air, in real time. This dynamic repeats itself in cycles throughout the day until everyone staggers out of the newsroom broken and spent—their finite attention capacity depleted.

On other days, however, there are not a lot of newsworthy events to report. As a result, journalists are spared the usual manic, overextended workload. There is a familiar term for this: the "slow news day." Slow news days inspire a mix of relief and ennui among the journalists. On one hand they are viewed as random and fortuitous reprieves from the chaos. But because the apotheosis of news production is the live breaking event, and because newsroom cultures encourage panicked overwork and adrenaline rushes to service that ritual, some journalists feel that they are not alive, and indeed the world is not turning, if something seemingly earth-shattering is not being reported. So like miners who have extracted every ounce of ore from a mountainside and continue to look for more, the news producers double or triple their efforts to dredge up anything that smacks of novel to feed into the machine. I once worked with a producer who, eyeing the possible eruption of a war along the tense border between North and South Korea, expressed her hopes out-loud that fighting would erupt, allowing the show to go into breaking news mode and thus put an end to the slow news day that was keeping her—and presumably her audience—too calm.

The slow news day, unfortunately, tends to be the exception. More normally, we are manically managing the mess. And because human beings are a talented, adaptive and resourceful species capable of profound achievements, the mess *is* managed, and the news is produced. Yet what is the price we pay as a society in terms of the quality of what is churned out? A kind of fast food for the collective consciousness?

CAPTURE AND HOLD

THE MAIN OBJECTIVE of every news factory is to capture our attention, and in some cases to try and hold it for as long as possible. They do so to garner ratings, clicks and subscriptions which it sells back to advertisers. The news includes and excludes content based on what might work best to grab and lock our attention—sex, violence, crime, perversion, wars, natural disasters, political and celebrity scandals and adorable things like cute cuddly animals. The mere structure of a TV news broadcast—the stacking and sequencing of many stories, one following the other—has the effect of pulling viewers back into the show time and again, as if from the start.[1]

Cable TV news stations use a slew of other methods to help draw-in viewers and keep them watching. More obvious gambits include the short but seductively scripted promotional segments that run before commercial breaks announcing what's "coming up"—and why you need to keep watching. Other techniques fall below our radar of what constitutes a sales pitch. By design the news is presented in a carnival of kaleidoscopic signals meant to impress, dazzle and hypnotize us into a suggestive state. They include moving banners with provocative titles, gyrating lights, tickers, wipes, theme music and other colourful special effects. Teams of graphics professionals are drawn upon daily to create and add new bling to a show's audio-visual repertoire.

Employing music is the easiest way to manipulate human emotions. BBC World News precedes its broadcast with a dramatic countdown that crescendos in ominous drumbeats preceding each headline which is read in a dire tone at the top of the show. Similarly, the news wings of the major TV networks in the United States try to convey an air of officialdom through the use of dramatic opening theme music. Patriotic and state anthem-style trumpets used by NBC and ABC news broadcasts are meant to project authority, as if heralding the king before a pronouncement or decree. Voice of God introductions of news anchors that begin with "From world headquarters..." or "From the nation's capital..." are also meant to jack-up credibility.[2]

And of course, there is the increasingly ubiquitous designation applied to evermore stories: 'BREAKING NEWS.' The red coloured bannering, employed universally across all TV news organizations, screams 'Emergency!' 'This is important!' and 'Pay attention!' Incidentally it is the same colour that Instagram, LinkedIn, Facebook and other social media platforms use on their dashboards to announce new likes, messages and other dopamine-triggering offerings that help addict us and ensure user engagement. Breaking news *is* the pinnacle and essence of the news production experience. But in their desperation of late to remain economically viable, news organizations now overplay the breaking news card.[3] The habit of doing so has rendered breaking events increasingly meaningless.

As a television news writer I have helped produce scores of breaking news stories. Perhaps it says something when I tell you that, with a few notable exceptions, I have forgotten nearly all of them.

THE ERRORS OF OUR WAYS

This is the heart of modern journalism, the rapid repackaging of largely unchecked second-hand material.
    – Nick Davies, *Flat Earth News*

IN THE FRENETIC environment I have described, it's hard to imagine accuracy *not* becoming a casualty. And it usually does. In the newsroom, mistakes—most of them small, a few others larger—are ubiquitous. I should know: I made loads of them in my time as a TV news writer. They include things like spelling mistakes in copy and in banners, inaccurate numerical figures, and even wrong or outdated video footage (a map used in a recent Fox News TV broadcast placed the Upper Peninsula of Michigan in Canada). The types of possible screw-ups are too many to list. Journalists, being human and invariably over-worked, are going to commit errors. Inaccuracy is thus an unavoidable reality of the news business just as it is unavoidable for army soldiers to be injured, or killed, during the course of a war. When news budgets and resources are slashed and reporter workloads increase as a result, so do the errors. As a result, *almost all* major stories carry some manner of inaccuracy at some point during their coverage life. They vary between the minor cosmetic flaws like the ones I have listed to entire premises that are outright false because their source was unreliable.

One good example of the latter was a January 2018 story about a young Muslim girl in Toronto who said she was attacked twice on the way to school by a man who cut her hijab with scissors. That incident which made headlines around the world, drew a firestorm of condemnation from the general public and government officials, including the Canadian Prime Minister. But the story turned out to be untrue: the young girl later admitted to making it up.

Oops.

Luckily, many errors are caught in the newsroom and fixed before most of the public sees them. When they aren't nabbed in time, print and online publications will often carry a retraction after the fact. In more serious cases, journalists can be fired as happened in September 2017, when CNN dismissed three reporters from its elite *CNN Investigates* team who reported inaccurate information on Trump's alleged collusion with Russia. The retracted article was one of a series of damaging reporting errors made by that unit over time.

There is an old saying that 'a lie can travel halfway around the world while the truth is putting on its shoes.' The quote is applicable to how inaccuracy in one news story can spread across the entire media landscape faster than a wind-stoked wildfire. One example stands out.

In August 2015, British newspapers *The Mail, Telegraph, Metro* and television news channel *Sky News* reported a story that came via the wire service *Agence France Press* about the death of a young South Asian girl in Dubai who had drowned at the beach after her father stopped lifeguards from performing life-saving measures on her. The religiously conservative dad apparently didn't want the men to physically touch his daughter. After the news item went viral around the world, an equally shocking—and deeply telling—revelation came to light. It was discovered that the story first appeared in a United Arab Emirates publication called *Emirates* 24/7. It took the form of an anecdote in an interview with a member of the Dubai Police Search and Rescue Department who recounted the incident after being asked what the strangest thing was that had ever happened to him on the job. *The drowning incident he related, that was being reported as news, took place back in 1996.* The original *Emirates* 24/7 article indicated that it was an old incident.

The British newspaper that first ran the story, trusting that AFP did due diligence, likely didn't look into the story further. The other papers, which followed suit, in the U.K. and around the world, also took it for granted that the story was accurate as reported.

This is an example *par excellence* of "lazy journalism" and the tendency by news organizations nowadays to rely too much upon the work of other new agencies and organizations. News factory culture is a copycat culture. All news organizations, to varying degrees, repackage each other's material in lieu of doing their own original, grass-roots reporting. This was also the case before the internet. But in the age of Google this tendency has exploded into a common bad habit.

During my own time in the television newsroom at CBC News Network the majority of the stories I worked on largely involved repackaged elements from other news organizations: Reuters, NBC, CNN, The Canadian Press, various newspaper websites, Twitter, Facebook, YouTube—anything. I had no direct connection to original sources for most stories I worked on, nor any objective knowledge of how true, or untrue, its elements were. Some reporters I worked with—either network or freelance—also had no direct link to the news they covered and simply read the same wire and online copy that I had. Nowadays, there are no budgets to pay for bureaus, travel and the gathering of original material. If you consider how much information on the web is either unverified and/or inaccurate, and that all news organizations incestuously 'copy-paste' from each other, you can see how a debacle like the one involving the Dubai story can occur.

Print and online editors and TV news script vetters, whose job it is to check work for accuracy and errors under strict deadlines, also do so partly by way of second-hand media sources—which have all been sharing the same information. If editors have specialized knowledge they may be able to catch a mistake, a half-truth, a misconception, or a word that implies something else. What they can't do is check if a story is fundamentally true to its core at every level—or if it actually happened as reported. There is simply not enough time and information available to do so.

DUMB AND DUMBER

Entertainment is the supra-ideology of all discourse on television. No matter what is depicted or from what point of view, the overarching presumption is that it is there for our amusement and pleasure.
  – Neil Postman, *Amusing Ourselves to Death*

Is it a problem that our mental representation of the world is the product of a for-profit entertainment industry? Yes.
  – Greg Jackson, "Vicious Cycles: Theses on a Philosophy of News"

ANYONE WHO'S FOLLOWED the news, especially for the last decade, has noticed without fail that coverage has tilted more and more towards stories about celebrities and all manner of trivial conflicts between members of the public. What was once the sole domain of what we call "tabloid" news has spread to become a fixture of many mainstream news outfits. Hardly a day goes by without an ultra-bizarre and deeply insignificant news item gracing our smartphone newsfeeds. "TWO CATHOLIC NUNS LEFT ITALY TO DO MISSION WORK IN AFRICA. WHEN THEY RETURNED, THEY WERE PREGNANT" ran one *National Post* headline that smacked more of salacious gossip than important news. The cumulative impact of these stories is that they dumb us down— not just as individuals, but as a culture. Why is this happening at all, and why now?

This epoch's most life-altering development, the birth of the internet, has ushered in a universe of competing news content— not just from master storytellers but also from poor imitators who have undercut the news giants. Pseudo-news sites like *Buzzfeed*, *Mashable*, *Upworthy*, and *The Huffington Post* quickly learned to out-sensationalize more reputable news organizations by featuring gossipy stories with loads of celebrity side-boob. Others with more journalistic bona fides like *Vice* simultaneously out-cooled the traditional news dinosaurs by more quickly embracing digital platforms and spinning a sub-genre of irreverent reporting catered to hipsters and millennials.

In the cable TV world, the hard slide into 'reality television' with its thoughtless yet titillating shows featuring Kardashians, American Idols, and Apprentices, joined hands with Showtime's and HBO's higher quality dramatic series to take a big bite out of the entertainment market. Netflix, of course, has since shot to first place in the great entertainment game with its endless offerings to win us over. Amazon Prime and Apple TV came next. To top it off there is the endless stream of all other internet and social media content, which taken together, can constitute its own veritable newsfeed and window on the world.

There has never been more entertainment available to keep

us distracted and preoccupied. To compete and survive, *the corporate news media has had to up its game, paradoxically, by lowering its game.*

This hard tilt towards the news as entertainment is not entirely a new development. Historically, as the news increasingly co-opted visual media and methods into their storytelling —starting with photos in newspapers and then later film and later video footage in TV news broadcasts—it has increasingly moved away from a rational, typographic culture to one which is image-centred, emotional and pleasure driven.

The world of celebrities, the closest thing to a pantheon of gods we revere in our secular culture, are the low-hanging fruit of news—and the most easily consumable by the population, including the young (the hardest demographic for the newsmongers to hook). Even once-stalwart and respectable news giants like the BBC News and CBS's news magazine show *60 Minutes* have buckled under the pressure to feature the exploits of the rich, famous and infamous. A *60 Minutes* interview, in March 2018 with American porn actress Stormy Daniels who purportedly took hush money over an alleged affair with Donald Trump, attracted 22 million viewers. It was the show's best ratings since a 2008 segment on the Obamas ratcheted over 24 million American viewers.

I've seen my own television newsroom at CBC News Network become infected over time by this tendency to feature celebrity stories. I was working on the day that the U.K.'s Prince Harry and American actress Meagan Markle suddenly announced their engagement in 2017. The entire day's newscast was hijacked by disproportionate coverage featuring royal watchers and fashion commentators sharing rumours and speculations about the upcoming wedding, as lower third banners ran beneath them reading: "MARKLE ENGAGEMENT DRESS BOASTS REPORTED $95K PRICE TAG" and "THE ONE OF A KIND ROYAL RING." When later, in 2020, the same news organization ran a story about Peter Phillips—a largely unknown grandson of Queen Elizabeth—becoming divorced from his Canadian wife, more than a few staffers were scratching their heads in the newsroom wondering why this was a story.

So desirable is celebrity content that even somewhat forgotten people who were once famous, or had the most fleeting brush with fame, such as former American Idol contestants or Whitney Houston's daughter's ex-boyfriend, make the news when they die. Similarly, lots of crime stories appeal to news producers for the added reason that the criminals involved become instant celebrities—but of the news media's making. It may even be that in some cases the would-be criminals commit crimes, in part, *to become* celebrities since they know the news will turn them into icons of a sort.

Pettiness and triviality are the handmaidens of news that aims to appeal to the emotions. It's what the American linguist and social critic Noam Chomsky calls "marginalia"—inconsequential information which serves to distract us from what is important. News organizations have always on occasion churned out insignificant stories. But in the digital age the *amount* of content that is potentially publishable online on any given day is much greater than it was during the print era. News operations make use of what is, in theory, unlimited space. This can have positive implications like providing coverage to stories that once wouldn't make the cut because of space or time limitations. But it also allows news organizations to flood the market with chaff. They now feed an insatiable online beast with almost any content in order to compete, not just with each other, but with *all* other web and social media offerings. This desperate behaviour means that any news that smacks of the odd, the bizarre, the twisted, the silly or the marginally divisive including but not limited to things like petty crimes, viral videos, social media outrages and incidents of political incorrectness, now make the cut. Triviality and stupidity are routinely elevated to matters of importance and celebrated. Newsroom workers have become conditioned to this prime directive and now wait— like a cat crouched in ambush outside a mousehole—for the next potential outrage.

When Canadian musician Jocelyn Alice let out a mirthful giggle while singing Canada's national anthem at the 2017 Major League Baseball All-Star game, bored and conflict-prone members of the public took to Twitter to attack her, saying she had debased the anthem. Her giggle (more of a live performance chortle) was hardly out of place, if at all noticeable. Yet CBC News Network seized on the Twitter feedback and featured the "story" in its early morning broadcast. The promotional bump for it, running before the commercial break, gives an idea of the sort of "news" Canadians can nowadays sometimes wake up to:

"Coming up... It's the giggle heard all the way from Miami. Last night during the MLB All-Star opening ceremony, Canadian singer-songwriter Jocelyn Alice let out a very noticeable giggle during the national anthem. And the backlash against the moment has been swift. So it got us thinking—should we do away with singing anthems at sporting events? We're hearing from you and we'll share some of those responses..."

This sort of triviality obfuscates what's really going on. In the online world those consequences are amplified by the news media's use of "most shared," "most emailed," or "most read" lists on their websites, which ensure that the sensational stories dominate the pile, getting even more visibility and clicks at the expense of others. This creates a feedback loop which incentivizes frippery. In the TV realm producers are then encouraged to cover those same top web stories, because of their popularity.

These market-driven decisions to prioritize trivia over deep significance work to change societal norms of what is important in the world. Audiences are conditioned and brainwashed by this content which not only dumbs down our culture, but also dangerously polarizes it.

TRUMPING THE REAL STORY

They are puppeteered by their own game, caught in a bind whereby their abhorrence of Trump and their audience's abhorrence of Trump elevated him to such cacophonous prominence that he had a shot of winning the presidency. And when he did win and the mood among reporters at the New York Times turned bleak, the paper's executive editor, Dean Baquet, was surprised at the response: this was the story of a lifetime.

> – Greg Jackson, "Vicious Cycles: Theses on a Philosophy of News"

THE SINGLE GREATEST object lesson about the *modus operandi* of the news media and its impact on reality is in its relationship to Donald J. Trump and his presidency. Without doubt there were numerous factors at play in the real-estate tycoon's capture of the White House. People may disagree on how to rank those in order of magnitude or importance, but one thing is nearly impossible to deny: news organizations, with CNN leading the way, were crucial in elevating the man to the presidency.

When I noticed the amount of airtime the U.S. TV networks were giving Trump in the earliest days of his run for the Republican Party leadership, and how well he performed for them, I knew he was likely to win. It must have been a no-brainer for TV news executives to decide to shine the spotlight on him—and keep it there. And how could they resist? He ticked every single box for what constitutes, in the jargon of the broadcast news business, "great TV." He was a famous celebrity who was well-trained, from years of reality-television appearances, to perform before the camera. He was controversial, charismatic, rude, off-the-cuff and sometimes funny. It didn't matter that he was a political neophyte and business charlatan who blathered a lot of empty words. He promised to be the story that keeps on giving: a guaranteed four years of sensational and unprecedented headlines to help pull news organizations out of the financial gutter.

In February 2016, during the Republican leadership race, the then president of CBS, Leslie Moonves, speaking about Trump and the spike in political advertising revenue CBS garnered from his campaign and that of his competitors, said of the Trump phenomenon, "It may not be good for America, but it's damn good for CBS." In November 2018, after Trump became president, Jeff Zucker, the president of CNN (who also helped Trump get started on TV when he green-lit *The Apprentice* as the head of NBC) shared similar enthusiasm for the Trump story in a *Vanity Fair* interview when he said, "We've seen that anytime you break away from the Trump story and cover other events in this era, the audience goes away," he added. "So we know that, right now, Donald Trump dominates."

When the TV people decided to back their man with all that attention, everyone else followed suit. Both the *New York Times* and *Washington Post*, for example, have experienced huge spikes in their subscriptions and the revivals of their brands by dedicating their domestic political coverage to debunking Trump at any and every turn.[1] The rest, of course, is history. Trump's tendency to attack, demean, and bully his opponents and to create scandalous controversies that draw attention to himself were seized by news organizations and made into one years-long news event.

The news media and the erstwhile U.S. President were locked in an awkward and complex dance. The former at once appear to revile him on the surface yet they supported his celebrity cult by virtue of the amount of obsessive coverage they gave him. News organizations scrambled to feature his tweets like Pavlov's dogs responding to a bell. The same goes for Trump. He claims to hate most media, calling them "fake news" at every turn, yet he constantly played to and relied on them to draw evermore attention to himself. The result was the creation of a new type of high-stakes reality television series that came to hijack real life; a living and breathing Netflix or HBO-style soap, whose consequences reverberated across the real world.

Countless other news stories have been lost or underplayed because of the obsession with Trump's monkey business. As Noam Chomsky, and others, have reminded us periodically, every time Trump gave the news media a new outrage—possibly, at times, deliberately—the frantic and hysterical coverage of those events served to eclipse other important political stories about the re-engineering of American society: whether it's at the hands of Trump's cabinet members, or by Congress, or by the President himself.[2] As a news service, if you were too busy focussing on Trump's petty feuds, or on his latest shocking tweet, you not only reinforced Trump's behaviour and unnecessarily agitated the masses, but you also excluded other important news which could have taken its place. This corruption and failure of journalism is a huge story in its own right—one that the media also conveniently ignores.

FEW EXPERTS HERE

Journalists have to pretend to know everything about everything. In fact (though please do not broadcast this) they know surprisingly little about many things.
  – Philip Howard, *The Press Gang: The World in Journalese*

Many newspaper stories are inaccurate when judged by those who know something about the issue being discussed.
  – Chapman Pincher, *Inside Story: A Documentary About the Pursuit of Power*

NEWS PROFESSIONALS TEND to be generalists when it comes to understanding the stories they cover. Their familiarity with topics can be very broad indeed, but as self-proclaimed "news junkies" much of their knowledge tends to come from watching the news over a lifetime—and thus can reflect many of the ideas and clichés the news media has always propounded about the world.

Real, intricate, living expertise across a wide range of topics is hard to find in any given newsroom, let alone in any journalist. Reporters and writers occasionally do bring valuable specialized knowledge that bridges the expertise gap by way of their cultural backgrounds, former careers, hobbies, or time spent living in a certain parts of the world. Exceptionally talented veteran journalists and correspondents who cover specific beats and move in the social and professional circles of their chosen specialization can also bring additional knowledge to the news game. But many of the rank-and-file news workers are by and large generalists.

As a result, many journalists and their editors may work on stories they know little, or nothing, about. They can hardly be relied upon to consistently bring a more a critical and nuanced eye to stories with complex or esoteric aspects to them: whether they be scientific, technological, legal, racial or cultural in nature. Even reporters who have much experience in a certain beat, say, national security or diplomatic correspondents, still have not worked *in* those fields and usually don't know what insiders in those professions understand at a core level (in part, too, because they lack security clearance). The problem is it often takes the right expert with serious inside knowledge of a subject to point out errors and misconceptions—and overlooked subtleties—that result in a story being simplified and misconstrued.

For instance, in spite of all the news coverage in recent years about possibly sending astronauts—including (in Elon Musk's imagination) around one million people—to settle Mars, we seldom, if ever, hear from anyone in the news that radiation-levels on the red planet are too high to sustain human life there. It takes certain scientists in possession of that knowledge to point that out.

Sources, interviewees and pundits can and do sometimes fill-in these knowledge gaps successfully (as do newsrooms with a greater diversity of staff)—but the person you're interviewing must have a sufficient degree of insight and experience to give their statements worth. Some pundits are simply armchair "experts" and academics—more self-proclaimed gurus in a field than bona fide authorities whose knowledge has been culled from books and research. Much reporting about little-known countries and cultures, such as Iran and North Korea, has been deeply skewed because of an almost total first-hand inexperience of those places.[1] Similarly, no one can speak meaningfully about Russia or China, which are infinitesimally complex and hard to penetrate cultures, by simply analyzing surface events there from afar. Anyone who claims to speak with authority about a country or culture they've never spent time immersed in, let alone visited, is at best just repeating things that someone else has said.

When media sources *do* have access to crucial expertise, the generalist machinery of the news factory may, or may not, heed it. A few notable examples involve the anthrax biological weapons scare of 2001 and the subsequent post-9/11 fears about foreign terrorists detonating a "dirty bomb" (a small, crude homemade explosive device that could be employed to spread radioactive material in a city). Fearful and lazy reporting by journalists who knew little about the science around those issues helped create societal angst. News organizations seldom featured the more intelligent and sobering expertise that downplayed—or debunked—the catastrophe scenarios tied to the use of both of those tools as weapons. In the case of anthrax spores, they are highly ineffective as a biological weapon. The illness it causes is non-infectious and treatable with antibiotics. The potency of anthrax spores decreases when exposed to sunlight, air currents, and certain temperatures, and thus don't make for a reliable weapon. Likewise, the successful assembly, construction and delivery of a small, mobile "dirty bomb" was not only deemed highly unlikely because of the technological expertise required for it, but would have caused little damage, either physical or radiological. Yet we almost never heard those views because the hypothetical horror stories were more entertaining; and thus more effective in capturing the public's imagination and attention—the news media's prime directive.

More recently when devastating wildfires caused widespread destruction across parts of the Pacific Northwest region of North America in the summers of 2018 and 2020 (a now more frequent trend resulting partly from hotter, dry summers), news organizations predictably focussed on both the human dramas created by the blazes—and the climate change angle. The latter is treated as the sole aggravating factor for the increase in fires. To be sure climate has been a considerable factor. Somewhat cooler, wetter weather, which was more recently the norm in the northwest, does not result in uncontrollable fires of that magnitude. But an important component of that story was largely bypassed in the rush to drama stoked by the emotionally-charged climate change angle. Those fires are also the result of poor forest management practices for over half a century. Decades of suppression of naturally-occurring and regenerative wildfires have resulted in weaker, diseased and more combustible forests. That combined with widespread clear-cutting of more fire-resistant old growth trees and their replacement with second growth species has also greatly contributed to the blazes. Years of bark beetle infestation, which has killed countless trees, has only added to the mass of fire kindling that exists in the form of logging slash.[2]

Friends and acquaintances I know in British Columbia, Canada, who have a deep and intimate knowledge of forestry issues complained that news organizations don't mention enough how these factors are contributing to the wildfires. Most big city journalists in Toronto or New York, unacquainted as many of them are with their hinterlands, don't even realize that there is more to know about a topic like this. It was only in the autumn of 2018 year, after the fires abated, that an important online story highlighting such forest management practices in British Columbia, and its impact on wildfires, ran on the CBC News website. There has been subsequent mention of these factors in the other print and online media, yet it remains largely unexamined in the more entertainment-driven television news media.

VIGILANCE MISDIRECTED

> *... a culture that exemplifies the qualities of the left hemisphere's work attracts to itself, in positions of influence and authority, those whose natural outlook is similar... Thus a culture which already has some prominent autistic characteristics attracts to positions of influence individuals who will help it ever further down the same path.*
>
> – Iain McGilchrist, *The Master and His Emissary*

ALL THINGS CONSIDERED, newsrooms *do* work hard to try to keep their coverage accurate, ethical and integral—by their own definitions of course. The problem is that they approach the task in a narrow and reductionist way. The focus is on the smaller details of the content and operation. Is a story 'balanced'? Should a certain person be named? Is running with an allegation actually abetting possible slander? Is the spelling in a banner correct? Is this sentence too passive in tense?

This narrow focus means that news organizations eschew

bigger picture considerations. At best managers might explore how to better adapt to long-term technological trends to grow their audiences, or emulate their more sensational news competitors. But they seldom if ever deeply question themselves philosophically about who they are, what they are about, and what they are actually doing. As far as I know there is no deep soul-searching to determine if the work they produce is actually news, whether that content is *fundamentally* important or ethical in a big picture sense, and what its overall impact on society might be. News operations are blind and negligent in these areas. For this reason much of what this book attempts to highlight seldom falls on their radar. And there are reasons for this that are more common to the human condition than are specific to journalists working in organizations (and their controllers).

Highlighting deep truths and exposing problematic practices within the news game is fundamentally inconvenient for everyone involved. It disrupts the standard operating procedures and workflow in the news factory. Approaching work mindfully with the intention of improving it creates *more* work and triggers passive-aggressive responses among and between colleagues and their superiors. Making suggestions for real positive change might also endanger your job and the ultimate golden calf: the retirement pension. As a result even if morale in the newsroom is low (which it often is) and there is much reason to improve the operation, few people will speak-up and rock the boat.

Organizational self-improvement is also elusive because newsrooms are by their very nature more left-brained, and, especially in the case of TV, demonstrate certain autistic traits.[1] An important explainer: our brains evolved left and right hemispheres from a need to manage two different mental tasks at once. One is to focus on details—such as a bird does when it searches for food on the ground. The other is to scan more broadly and be cognizant of possible dangers and opportunities in the wider environment. Those tasks require two distinct and separate ways of seeing the world. Generally, the right brain specializes in seeing the bigger picture. Of necessity it is more contextual and holistic in view. It is also attuned to meaning. The left brain is more computer-like. It is detail-oriented, linear, analytical, reductionist and dualistic. Ideally both hemispheres work in a somewhat balanced fashion. But hard news operations draw far more upon the left-brain tendencies. Not only do newsrooms specialize in finding and highlighting events that are largely devoid of deeper context and meaning, they also separate and focus on a cluster of events to the exclusion of all others —yet another culling of the bigger picture. It's a tunnel vision way of seeing that seeks to highlight minutiae and which breaks the world down to its smaller, component parts and details, without afterwards trying to synthesize them back into the whole. The tight deadlines, the panic-driven work rushes, and the factory-style production further narrows that tunnel-like focus that both draws from—and feeds—the left brain. Wider considerations become imperceptible.

The news wings of big public sector organizations like the BBC, or CBC, though they produce news, are still in essence bureaucracies. These work cultures tend to favour and reward ambitious and obsessive left-brained people who thrive while spinning on the hamster wheel. Is it any surprise that news outfits have devolved to highlight trivialities rather than seeking out deeper levels of context and profundity in their storytelling?

These mental habits not only trickle down into content but

are shaped by the demands of the tasks themselves. Copy vetters, who are the lower-level gatekeepers of TV news, are naturally fanatical about dotting the i's and crossing the t's. Ensuring clean and accurate copy is their game. Their bibles are the style and language guides of their particular organizations, which they sometimes commit to heart. They'll wring their hands and make a fuss about whether the acronym should contain periods (as in U.S. for United States) when appearing in a banner, or whether a word like "practice" should instead be spelled "practise," depending on its usage. To be fair, it is part of their job as editors. But attention to detail can and does, at times, go too far—no hairsplitting can be too microscopic. Nitpicking squabbles in the newsroom, sometimes lasting days, have erupted over how exactly to pronounce an ethnic surname, or whether to use a certain word over another which may have the slightest undesirable association with something else in meaning. By comparison, you seldom hear journalists seriously challenge their superiors or colleagues by saying, "Why are we running this story? This is sensationalism that is of no importance to anyone. Why don't we axe it?"

Obsessive tinkering with the parts in the newsroom shifts our attention away from the big questions that matter the most every single day:

What are we doing?
Why does this matter?
What are the implications?

DELIBERATE DISTORTION?

MANY OF US, at one time or another, have heard conspiracy theories about how the news media is run by a shadowy cabal of global untouchables that want to control information for their own political and economic ends. From my experience there is no evidence of that. There are no nefarious Illuminati puppeteers pulling the strings of the news media from some-where up-high. The vast majority of distortion in corporate news derives largely from practises and pressures stemming, as described, from a certain work culture, including by behaviours that occur largely outside of awareness.

That is not to say that journalists and their managers do not sometimes perpetrate more conscious forms of distortion. Ideo-logical bias infects every news organization. Media which tend to lean more 'left,' as, for instance, CBC News in Canada and *The Guardian* in the U.K., to name just a few, see the world through their own increasingly progressive lenses that nowadays prioritize issues involving identity, equality and rights and frame those topics in the wider picture of power struggles between establishment 'haves' who are guilty of perpetrating injustices against marginalized 'have-nots.' A friend who works as a diplomat and whose job involves scanning the headlines of several prominent global news organizations remarked to me recently that some liberal media outlets, including France 24 English, CNN International and BBC World, "can behave more like civil society advocacy NGOs than news organizations." That editorial slant undoubtedly reflects one aspect of life, but when news is repeatedly filtered through that worldview with its attendant heroes, villains and victims, you get a skewed picture of reality.

So too with 'right-wing' and 'ultra-conservative' media organizations, such as the Fox News in the United States, or some Postmedia publications in Canada, which cast a different set of villains, heroes, and victims. Their depictions tend to reflect a world in which people holding traditional values, including individual rights, are oppressed by an intellectual elite that seeks to reshape culture based on academic notions that are divorced from a more common-sense understanding of the world. Here too there are seeds of truth, but as the sole paradigm for understanding the world it is overly simplistic—and sometimes elevates ideas that are more appropriate to the past (such as some conservative attitudes on the U.S. constitutional right to keep and bear arms). Both narratives clash, but are also intertwined and feed off each other. But these biases, even if their purveyors are conscious of them as such, are still reflections of what journalists take to be reality, and therefore don't qualify as efforts to deliberately misinform in the sense of consciously lying. People are simply reporting the world as they see and understand it. And there are, of course, journalists on either side of that ideological divide who try to be more nuanced, or open-minded, in their portrayals.

More deliberate politically-motivated distortion does occur among some media outlets. The 24-hour English-language station Russia Today (RT) and Breitbart News Network produce stories with staggeringly disproportional bias (Fox News can sometimes be included here). That temptation to "cook the books" can occur even in the best news outfits, albeit less frequently. I witnessed such moments in 2015 when I worked in the television newsroom of Al Jazeera English (AJE) in Doha, Qatar. I'll first say that Al Jazeera is one of the better news organizations I've had the pleasure to work for—as both a TV and freelance web journalist. They provide an inestimable service by reporting from countries and regions in the world where few, if any, other major news organizations tread, giving the otherwise invisible people of those places a voice with global reach. Their quality journalism, including their longer form reporting, is of the variety that wins prestigious awards. On the flip side, Al Jazeera is owned by the Qatari royal family and state, which has deep implications for its coverage of the Arab World. Its flagship Arabic-language service, which later spawned its sibling, AJE, has been a player in Middle Eastern politics since its inception. The news service has been described by some as a foreign policy tool of the Qatari government. Qatar threw its weight in support of the Sunni uprising in Syria while I worked at the station. AJE catered its coverage to reflect its political position—to the extent of avoiding blatant criticism of the more violent and fanatical anti-Assad rebel groups, including ISIS.[1]

Because Qatar was allied closely with Turkey in that effort to overthrow the Assad regime in Damascus, AJE also avoided any coverage that criticized Ankara.[2] News managers did the bidding of the higher-ups to that effect. Story pitches critical of

Turkey were repeatedly sidestepped or rationalized-away in editorial meetings. Managers also routinely monitored sensitive stories relating to the Sunni-Shia struggle in the region— whether in Syria, Yemen or beyond—and sometimes intervened to spin them to more strongly reflect the Sunni perspective, going as far as rewriting the news copy themselves at the last minute before the broadcast went to air. When the Saudi-led coalition air war against Yemen was launched in March 2015 (in which Qatar was involved), the station went into war-room mode with the nervous managers constantly looking over our shoulders and making editorial redactions to make sure the political message was on point (the entire broadcast team from London was flown to Qatar temporarily so that management could direct control of their work in-person).

Yet interestingly, when Doha fell-out politically with Saudi Arabia and the United Arab Emirates in June 2017, AJE's broadcasts became critical of the war in Yemen.

GROUPTHINK
WHEN NO ONE SPEAKS OUT

Has there ever been a society which has died of dissent?
Several have died of conformity in our lifetime.
— Jacob Bronowski in "Science and Human Values"

IN NOVEMBER 2018, the *Ottawa Citizen* newspaper reposted a video clip on its YouTube account showing members of the Ottawa Senators NHL hockey team in an Uber vehicle complaining to one another about the performance of their team and coach. The footage was secretly recorded by their driver and later appeared online. Soon after, most major news organizations in Canada, and beyond, aired the footage either on TV, and/or online. Apart from being trivial and journalistically irrelevant, the conversation was private and was recorded without the players' consent. But because news organizations are often on the lookout for gossipy, scandalous and celebrity content— and because it involved Canada's favourite sport and national pastime—little thought seemed to have been given to the journalistic and ethical merits of running the "story."

I was working at CBC News Network the day that news aired in the morning hours. "HIDDEN VIDEO AIRS SENS' DIRTY LAUNDRY," read the banner as the video ran—which was inaccurate since the Uber driver *and* news organizations were the ones *airing* the dirty laundry. When I asked co-workers what they thought about it, a few agreed that running the video was both problematic and in bad taste. Even the Uber driver, who was fired over the incident, later apologized for posting the video, which he admitted was a poor decision. But others didn't seem to think anything was wrong. "It's low-lying fruit," one colleague admitted. "But at the end of the day it sells. And no one is negatively affected except maybe those players." A few more colleagues shrugged their shoulders and carried on.

I was taken aback not only by the lack of professionalism becoming of real journalists, but also a conditioned herd mentality devoid of any free or critical thinking. Like the old story of the fish that has no idea it is in water because it is always surrounded by it, entire newsrooms have become largely unconscious of the extent to which the bar in the quality of their coverage has dropped over time. When individuals do occasionally awaken to it, not enough effort is made to seriously question those decisions, for the kinds of reasons I've mentioned. As a result, the limits of what is acceptable keep widening incrementally. Over time the damage to content and professional integrity becomes considerable.

In the early 1970s, Irving Janis, an American research psychologist and professor, popularized the term "groupthink" to describe the systematic errors committed by people when making collective decisions. Human groups tend to isolate themselves from outside influences and suppress dissenting and alternative viewpoints in order to maintain cohesion, minimize conflicts and reach consensus. This is bolstered by our propensity, as individuals, to keep ourselves in good standing in the groups we belong to. It's an evolutionary survival skill meant to keep us from being rejected and cast out. Because of these dynamics, people in groups tend to think alike. There is often little or no dissent. And that deliberate detachment from other perspectives and options means our thinking and actions tend to become fixed. The ability to be flexible is hamstrung and bad decisions result. The current tabloidization we're seeing in mainstream news occurs and is maintained partly because of groupthink.

Contrary to what my colleague said about no one but the players being negatively affected by the airing of the Senators' hockey video, there *are* wider consequences resulting from what happens in the newsroom—chief among them, the debasing of society. These real world implications affect all of us outside the hermetically sealed news factories whose purpose it is to *represent* the world; an environment ironically cut off from the very world it is reporting on. More than ever, newsrooms are self-enclosed realms that report on a world observed more virtually and conceptually than intimately and first-hand.[1] That and pressure to toe the line from within only adds another distorting effect to the picture they paint.

NEWS AFFECTIVE DISORDER (NAD)
THE COST TO OUR HEALTH

I have long lived with the unnerving feeling that we in the business of journalism are, by inadvertence, making people crazy.
  – Michael Enright, CBC Radio host

It's an ill office to be the first to herald ill.
  – Aeschylus, *Persians*, 1, 253

THERE ARE consequences to everything we say and do. This applies as much to the behaviour of news organizations as to that of collectives and individuals whose actions journalists try to hold to account; perhaps more so in the case of media because of how all-pervasive and influential it has become. Journalist Michael Enright, the former host of CBC Radio One's *Sunday Edition*, pointed out in a recent online article that the neurotic and freneti-cally paced news cycle is helping to make us physically and psycho-logically unwell. It's a rare admission coming from within the field of journalism. But what Enright says is something most of us know deep down. It doesn't require great vision or imagination to see that an unrelenting flow of sensationalized and often negative information broadcast from all quarters can and will ripple across society, washing over us and doing damage to us in the process.

Hard news, the fast food of the information ecosystem, is generally not good for us, especially in large doses. Content that is tragic, frightening or outrageous, and set to repetitive loops throughout the day, or week, will make us negatively emotional, stressed and anxious—even if we don't necessarily feel it enough to recognize it. This was never more the case than during the COVID-19 pandemic when the news went into rapacious overdrive, churning out every permutation of coronavirus scare story while reporting little else and thereby creating a sense of impending doom. At the height of the first wave some news websites carried no recent stories at all apart from those about the pandemic. Almost everyone I know outside my workplace who still followed the news in any meaningful way reacted by largely tuning it out.

News can and does trigger the human limbic system—the parts of our brain that regulate emotional and survival responses. When we're walloped repeatedly by the news media's rendition of the world, a place where danger, tragedy and other malign forces lurk around every corner, we tend to feel powerless and helpless. Our view of the world becomes pessimistic and cynical. Because the news almost never hedges its coverage with sufficient context explaining that certain events might be rare, isolated or limited in impact, and because news journalists don't often explore what can be done about serious issues, it often feels as if we are without agency and that the world is about to end. Indeed, people prone to or suffering from depression are very often specifically advised not to read, listen to or watch the news.

If the physical and mental health of the public is impacted as such, then what of the wellness of the journalists processing that information and doing the reporting? Those of us working in the newsroom are subject to the same negative emanations with all their potential health implications, but these may be amplified because we work with the raw materials at "ground zero." Newsroom workers channel these stories through themselves daily, not just as writers, editors and producers, but also as presenters and reporters who have to read or speak the stories and their associated jargon out loud every day.

As a result, journalists become trained and conditioned, to view the world in the narrow terms and perspectives defined by their industry.[1] Add the intense pressure cooker workflow with its juggling of stories, incessant deadlines, the flitting back and forth between various computer screens and applications, and the general culture of chaos and panic—all of which triggers the human fight-or-flight response—and it's not hard to see how news workers, in health-risk terms, are the coal miners of the modern-day office culture. Burnout is rife. Sick days are legion. Nervous breakdowns and more serious illnesses among the relatively young are not unheard of.[2] But equally destructive is the longer-term attrition level of the job that eats away at the soul, creating a kind of malaise that manifests as emotional indifference, which only the most resilient and dynamic personalities can barely keep at bay—and even then only for a time.

PART III

WHAT TO DO

We should remain at all times skeptically alert to the potentially gross idiocy that may lie concealed beneath the most beautiful fonts and the most authoritative and credible headlines. We should be as alert to media clichés as Flaubert was to literary ones. The latter ruin novels; the former can ruin nations.

– Alain de Botton, *The News*

HIGH STAKES

AN ACQUAINTANCE who has a much rosier view of the news media than I do recently asked me why when discussing the news business, I'm often critical.

"It's always the shortcomings you harp on," she complained.

You, the reader, may be thinking that too.

I have been focusing so far on what I deem to be broken or wrong because there is a deep crisis in the news industry. It is one which affects the way we see the world, thereby transforming the world, and impacts all of our lives—even those of us who have tuned the news out and think we have escaped it. It goes without saying that there is also much excellent and laudable work being done by news journalists. In spite of the ill-reputation we've earned within society, most of us are honest, hard-working and talented people. We would love as much as anyone to be employed in organizations that are not just functional, but are thriving and which allow us to do the best work possible—rather than being reduced to cogs in what are hidebound and dying entities. This, I think, is all the more reason to point out the weaknesses and try to improve things.

Some say that nothing of consequence can be done to salvage the industry. Those voices argue that the systemic factors and interests that drive mainstream news operations are too powerful to overcome. Journalist Nick Davies, whom I quote earlier, ends his book *Flat Earth News* by insisting that there is little, if anything, that can be done to ameliorate a news business infected by such decrepitude. In one sense he is correct: there is no quick and easy fix, no silver bullet, that can magically transform a rigid system that is woven into a larger and equally fixed disorder. The economic realities of the corporate news business and the human propensity to resist change and maintain the familiar and convenient attitudes towards work procedures are, on their own, nearly insurmountable difficulties.

I agree that the task is daunting and may seem as if it borders on the impossible. But we still need to try. The black-and-white attitude which states that because an undertaking is seemingly impossible to accomplish it should therefore not be attempted, fails to see that reaching for that goal may still generate dividends—regardless of the outcome. Striving for something seemingly beyond our reach and even "failing" in that task might still result in *some* change for the better. It needn't be an all-or-nothing proposition.

The industry should therefore buck the temptation to debase itself even further, and instead raise its game and become not just wiser, but more responsible and aware, otherwise our society becomes further compromised along with it. News consumers need to do the same, thereby helping to redefine the market and steer it away from the demand for shallow content—the journalistic equivalent of fast food. Our challenge is to lessen our addiction to news, question our response to it, and see how and why it can never tell the whole story. And that may serve us all.

Truly intelligent, nimble and forward-thinking news managers or executives would surely want to base their decisions on what is beneficial for society. In doing so they might also bring back into the fold those who have shunned the news for the intolerably trivial circus it has become. Rank and file journalists have a crucial bottom-up role to play here too.

If enough actions are taken in tandem, if enough voices are heard saying the same things over and over again, piecemeal changes could be made within any given newsroom.

SOME SUGGESTIONS FOR CHANGE

One key approach is to understand and then mitigate the dynamics and processes that contribute to distortion. Here are some suggestions for all of us working in the industry to consider.

1. Be service oriented. If we don't think a story can help our society better itself and thrive, let's reconsider running it. Where is society lacking? How can it be made more resilient and whole? And what is most *important* for people to know? We should make the case for and prioritize stories that speak to these questions and move beyond the narrow partisan obsessions of ideologues and dogmatists that we love to feature as storytellers because they're so divisive. News should be educational and insightful and geared towards helping us become better versions of ourselves.

2. Make journalism more solutions-based. News journalists would help matters considerably if they stop thinking, as often as they do, in a binary fashion: glorifying debate and regarding it as the best or only means of inquiry. This requires seeing the world less in black-and-white and either/or terms. Instead of reinforcing the zero-sum game built into irreconcilable conflict, let's seek the creation of new ideas that could help *resolve* those issues. The wider news media should be a forum where people don't necessarily argue, but also constructively explore and try to find solutions *together*—or at least admit that some issues transcend either 'left' or 'right' and can't be boiled down to two opposed positions. The criteria for a good guest or interviewee should not be a rigid viewpoint and dramatic combativeness, but the ability to see and articulate shades of grey and to generate templates for solutions.

3. Understand that most events don't have a single cause and are not simply the "fault" of one agency. Provoking shame and assigning blame are endeavours of the small-minded. We should eschew the tendency to choose a "villain" on which to focus blame—simply to appease the bloodthirsty masses. We journalists, when possible, should try to recognize and acknowledge the multifaceted and intertwined origins of the events we cover. If a protagonist or group featured in a story seeks to assign singular blame for an event with manifold origins, the news should challenge that notion where applicable. There can be no solutions-based journalism, or deeper understanding about the world, without knowledge of a bigger picture. Seeing that wider perspective prevents us from stirring up damaging negative emotions on which the blame game relies.

4. If you're a national news service, avoid elevating what should remain local stories, especially local crimes and their criminal trials, into big headlines just because they are considered sensational. Crime news that is too localized alienates wide geographical audiences as it's deemed to be irrelevant. If a local crime story is too big *not* to bring to wider attention, there is still no need for us to harp on it *ad infinitum* or make it a top headline. Alternately, local good news stories that demonstrate some exceptionality in people and in the human condition—and are thereby *inspiring*—will resonate far more widely than a crime ever can. News journalists have to dig harder, and sometimes do their own original journalism, to find them. But the benefits for society are worth the investment in energy.

5. In cable news, resist the urge to roll breaking news coverage except in the most urgent circumstances that directly impact most of us. In spite of the tragedy for the victims, families and affected communities, sensational acts of local violence, like mass shootings, don't justify the indefinite hijacking of entire news cycles. The psychological impact of crimes of this nature are acutely magnified by endless and emotionally-heated news coverage. It is also worth keeping in mind that the perpetrators, particularly mass-murderers and terrorists, will have factored media attention into their decision to commit the crime. Only if there is an unambiguous and practical need for a wide segment of society to remain informed about an unfolding event, should live breaking news continue roll. Similarly, it should not be used as a tool to generate voyeuristic entertainment.

6. Slow down. If a story requires more time to get proper treatment and to get its facts correct, it can wait to run. Let's create a news culture that can come to terms with that. Journalists will derive a deeper sense of meaning and satisfaction from their work if they know that they are doing a more thorough—and therefore better—job. Over time morale will increase. Sick days will drop. Those are good reasons for bosses to listen to us, to give us the time the story warrants and not rush us. There is nothing more daunting to journalists, damaging to a story, and disrespectful to an audience than an unreasonable deadline to complete an assignment.

7. Do more longer form journalism. News organizations should try to commission more lengthy text pieces in print and especially online (where financially feasible to do so). In television and radio, reporters should be allotted longer times for their live reports, packages and items. Extra storytelling space and time translates directly into more context and nuance. Depictions of reality become slightly less skewed as a result.

8. Widen hard news operations to include more current affairs stories. We need to open the door to slower journalism that doesn't have a hard news peg. Let's consider, including topics with non-traditional angles that highlight slower trends and developments that better represent reality—and which might thereby attract new audiences. Al Jazeera English excels at bringing viewers reports from very remote and unheard-of places in the world, and on topics that are not traditionally covered by mainstream news. "Good news" stories can often be of this variety.

9. Create a diverse newsroom. I don't mean diversity in just the narrower and politically-correct sense of "identity" which drives the pursuit of racial and gender equality targets in the workplace—although that should be part of the larger effort. News managers should instead cast their nets wider and strive for what author Matthew Syed in his book *Rebel Ideas* calls "cognitive diversity," or diverse thinking. News managers should seek out employees with different educations, backgrounds, life experiences and value systems from one another. Cognitive diversity, which is the proclivity of group members to think differently from one another about the world around us, is the critical ingredient in collective intelligence. Better ideas and better journalism are the fruits of that dynamic.

10. Break the groupthink. The longevity, livelihood and success of any organization rests to a significant degree on its ability to learn from the voices of constructive dissent and to admit its mistakes and act on them. Let's press our organizations to encourage dissenting views in the newsroom and allow journalists to speak freely and frankly about what they disagree with. Free and experimental thinking should be made part of the editorial process, even, and especially, if new ideas go against the sacred cows of the industry—or a particular news organization. Many original ideas may surface which would otherwise be suppressed because of fear of rejection and/or reprisal. Placing more flexible and non-traditional thinkers— rather than controlling personalities with orthodox views—in decision-making roles, will further this.

11. Speak up. As journalists we can make our voices heard at editorial meetings and encourage our colleagues to band together and do the same. Bring your own ideas to the table daily—especially stories that break the mould or go against the grain of what usually makes the cut.

12. Ask the public what they think of your news coverage—and listen to what they say. We can press television, radio and online platforms to create segments or sections that are equivalent to 'Letters to the Editor.' Broadcast programmes can be encouraged to create weekly panel interviews with informed and articulate members of the public to talk about how news stories were handled by the media— including their own—that week. News organizations have no issue with reporting Facebook and Twitter comments by the general public on other topics to jazz up their stories and to encourage greater interactivity with their online platforms. Why not feature real live humans talking openly about what they like and don't like about the news?

As individual journalists, we can also tap into the sentiments of the general public outside of work by way of our daily social interactions. If we repeatedly hear from friends, family and acquaintances that they no longer follow or watch the news because it is "too negative" or because it makes them feel "helpless" or "depressed" about the world, this is crucial information to relay to our bosses. The public's feedback on coverage of specific stories will help the operation to evolve.

It's not only journalists and news producers who can effect change here. So can the public. Daniel J. Boorstin, in his book, *The Image*, writes: "each of us individually provides the market and the demand for the illusions which flood our experience." Similarly, we news consumers can take actions to mitigate the impact the news has on our individual lives, and on our society. Here are a few suggestions:

1. Learn about the factors that influence how news is produced and how and why it affects us as it does. There are numerous articles, essays and books, including some referenced here, that critique the work of the corporate news media and describe its impact on society. Those can be found and sourced online. Sharing the ideas expressed in this, and other works, is part of that process.

2. Choose news sources that are more likely to look at the bigger picture, and less likely to harp on matters that are petty, trivial or otherwise insignificant. This includes deriving our "news" from longer form journalism—in-depth and well-researched stories that are not produced in a rush and which highlight slow, unobtrusive, and systemic trends that are all but invisible to the gatekeepers in the news business.

3. Break your addiction to hard news. Let's alternately attach and detach our attention from the news rather than incessantly monitor or binge on it. News addiction may not have the same stigma and effects as an addiction to alcohol, gambling or cocaine, but is still an addiction with highly unpleasant and undesirable side-effects including potentially: increased fear and anxiety, psychological conditioning as well as lost time and a depleted attention capacity. Not to mention a more skewed perception of reality.

4. Identify and avoid engaging with clickbait. If an online headline strikes you as absurdly petty and sensational, avoid the temptation to tap or click on it. In aggregate, this sends news organizations the message that we won't engage with the most meaningless of their fast-food offerings. It may also translate into less of that kind of material appearing in your social media feed.

5. Try to see any news story from as many different perspectives as possible, as opposed to just the one or two sides actually represented. Look at every news story as an incomplete portrayal of an event and try to imagine what other facts, perspectives or voices may be missing. Detaching emotionally while doing so will help free the mind from the narrower scope of vision that high emotional arousal creates. When we mitigate the conditioning effect the news has on us to see the world in two tones, we become more creative thinkers, and better problem-solvers and conflict managers.

6. Question the accuracy, relevance and importance of any given news story—even from the most reputable news organizations. As I hope I have shown, news is produced by imperfect humans, working in imperfect environments and with processes that are flawed. Always keep in mind that news is not gospel. It is seldom free of errors. Also note when a reported event is happening far removed from your immediate reality. Think about how uncommon, or rare, an occurrence mentioned in the news is. Consider whether any given story matters much in the grand scheme. And if a news story's headline is predicated on possibility, that something "may" or "might" happen, try reading the headline in the reverse: that it "may not" or "might not" happen, which is often just as likely. Question the assumptions that the news makes, and, just as importantly, question the assumptions that the news triggers in you.

7. Combine, contextualize and hedge any news with your own personal observations and experiences—and those of any informed contacts and networks. Often our experiences, and those of people we know, will contradict, or provide exceptions to what the news is telling us about the world.

8. Let news organizations know when they're lowering the bar with their coverage. Send a polite and elegantly written letter addressed to the relevant section or online editor or executive producer of a show. Don't carp and complain on social media. Everybody bitches on Twitter; it's expected and is considered cheap and ineffective. A letter is more powerful and will be taken more seriously. News organizations sell a product and they should be told by consumers when it is of unacceptably bad quality or below par.

9. Support journalistic projects and initiatives that seek to do things differently. Due to ailing finances, local news organizations across North America have been shutting their doors, depriving communities of both reporting that is more relevant to them—and a voice. There are a handful of organizations that are trying to promote and revitalize local journalism. The Knight Foundation, and its partners, for instance, support community journalism in the United States. We can do our bit to help them, and organizations like them. Other initiatives seek to bolster underrepresented genres and styles of journalism. Consider becoming a subscriber to *Delayed*

Gratification: The Slow Journalism Magazine. Or donate to *The Bureau of Investigative Journalism.* There are many such projects out there. We can share their work.

10. If you insist on remaining a 'news junkie,' at least become a more well-rounded news junkie by also consuming from sources that criticize and/or hold the media to account. The *Columbia Journalism Review* (CJR), a magazine published by Columbia University, and and Al Jazeera's show *The Listening Post* are two such examples.

Another approach for bringing about change in how we engage with "news" is to find evermore satisfaction in our own lives—in our work, hobbies and projects. When we are healthily engaged in undertakings that are genuinely satisfying and stretching, we are less prone to pettiness and seeking trivial stimulus from else-where—including from sensational news stories that are funda-mentally not relevant to our lives. Polemical, fear-inducing and/or tabloidy news is the "bread and games" of our age. The more we can free our thoughts and emotions from the loops of neuroses they might induce, the more capacity we have for seeing and appreciating the less thrilling, yet more holistic, shades of complexity about our world that might more reliably and accurately depict it.

As Alain de Botton writes, "A flourishing life requires a capacity to recognize the times when the news no longer has anything original or important to teach us; periods when we should refuse imaginative connection with strangers, when we must leave the business of governing, triumphing, failing, creating or killing to others, in the knowledge that we have our own objectives to honour in the brief time still allotted to us."

ENDNOTES

The News As Distortion

1. This, in contrast to spurious information shared online by the public in the form of misconceptions, rumours, opinions and conspiracy theories—all of which coalesce into a mass of falsehoods and which is sometimes included under the rubric of "fake news."

The Filter

1. Daniels, an adult film actress, claimed to have received money in return for signing a nondisclosure agreement before the 2016 U.S. presidential election about an affair she had with Donald Trump in 2006.

Exaggeration

1. Part of this is due to economics and expediency. Weather stories are cheap to produce and are good filler when other news runs thin.
2. Anyone familiar with American news coverage in the last few decades will know that political enemies are always dressed up in a way that is disproportionate to their reality. Saddam Husain, al-Qaeda, ISIS, Iran, North Korea, and, in some cases, Russia—although behaving malignly within their own spheres—have been portrayed as imminent, existential threats to the wider world. Journalist Glenn Greenwald, in *The Intercept*, writes that "journalistic standards are often dispensed with when it comes to exaggerating the threat posed by countries deemed to be the official enemy du jour. That is a journalistic principle that has repeatedly asserted itself, with Iraq being the most memorable but by no means the only example."

Who Doesn't Love a Good Story?

1. A 2009 study by the U.S. National Academy of Engineering and the National Research Council said that levees and flood walls surrounding New Orleans—no matter how large or sturdy—could not provide absolute

protection against overtopping or failure in extreme weather events. Instead, they should be viewed as a way to reduce risks from hurricanes and storm surges, not as measures that completely eliminate risk. As with any structure built to protect against flooding, the New Orleans hurricane-protection system promoted a false sense of security that areas behind the structures were absolutely safe for habitation and development.

2. Respected and world-renowned non-partisan scientists that question the need for the extent of the scaremongering and restrictions around COVID-19, and who offer more holistic policy approaches to navigate the pandemic (such as Carl Heneghan, Director of the University of Oxford's Centre for Evidence-Based Medicine, and Professor Sunetra Gupta, an infectious disease epidemiologist also at Oxford), are rarely featured in the corporate news media. News outfits also fail to properly contextualize the pandemic data, which contain enough skewing factors to render the numbers virtually meaningless on the surface, resulting in a misleading abstraction.

'The Argument Culture'

1. *Crossfire* was hosted by two pundits, one "on the left" and one "on the right," to represent both ends of the political spectrum. The show usually featured additional "left and right" guests during each topic of discussion.

2. It may not be a great stretch to say that the news media's obsession with stories of adversarial conflict places its product—in spirit—in a similar category to professional wrestling. I've actually heard more than one member of the public say as much, confirming my own thoughts on the matter.

3. The political polarization crisis in the U.S. involving Democrats and Republicans has been fuelled by the news media's obsession with framing their differences like a sports event. So too with Brexit in the U.K., and pipeline politics in Canada. When a public forum is created for two sides to ram heads and shout past one another, there can be no possibility for seeing a bigger picture.

Coloured by Numbers

1. Watch any cable TV news station and note how many pharmaceutical, insurance and health-related ads run during the commercial breaks.

2. "Our study shows that many biomedical findings reported by newspapers are disconfirmed by subsequent studies. This is partly due to the fact that newspapers preferentially cover "positive" initial studies rather than subsequent observations, in particular those reporting null findings. Our study also suggests that most journalists from the general press do not know or

prefer not to deal with the high degree of uncertainty inherent in early biomedical studies."

'Churnalism'

1. Social media will break some news faster than traditional news organizations.

Capture and Hold

1. The appearance of each new story in a broadcast is, in effect, an interruption —not unlike that which occurs with new messages and notifications on our smartphones. They disable our short-term memory and prevent us from properly digesting previous news items with a more discerning or critical eye.

2. Early evening broadcasts of ABC World News Tonight in the U.S. will sometimes preamble their headlines or newscast with the words "Tonight..." or "Just moments ago..." even when the events described happened earlier in the day. This is just another ploy to make the story appear breaking, and therefore newer when, in fact it's not. It's to ensure the viewer will remain glued to the broadcast.

3. Breaking news was held in reserve for the most monumental, history-making, events, which, before the birth of 24-hour cable TV news, came by way of dramatic interruptions (i.e. – "breaks") in "regularly scheduled programming" on television. Now the decision to brand a story as "breaking" is arrived at more willy-nilly.

Trumping the Real Story

1. A recent study has tracked how frequently the *New York Times* has cited the name "Trump" in its articles compared with other U.S. presidents going back to 1975. The NYTs mentions Trump 2–3 times as often as they did his presidential predecessors.

2. A great deal of environmental legislation, for instance, has been rolled-back under his tenure—a topic that's gotten very little media play compared with his personal shenanigans.

Few Experts Here

1. A list of American weekday cable TV news interviewees who most frequently appeared as guests in the aftermath the U.S. assassination of Iranian Major General Qassem Soleimani in January 2020, revealed that they were largely American military officers, academics, journalists, politicians and analysts. Of those none had speciality on Iran, only two were originally from the Middle East, and none were Iranian-American.
2. A marked increase in population, housing developments and human recreation in this region in recent years has also raised the incidents of fires being started and has put more people and property in the way of them.

Vigilance Misdirected

1. Blindness to context, a condition known as "caetextia," is the hallmark symptom and condition found across the autistic spectrum.

Deliberate Distortion?

1. There have been unsubstantiated accusations that elements within Turkey, Qatar and other Gulf countries had helped fund, arm and facilitate jihadist militias in Syria at the time, including possibly, if inadvertently, members of ISIS.
2. Al Jazeera English's reporting on Turkey during the 100th anniversary of the Armenian Genocide in 2015 was skewed in Turkey's favour. One news report about Turkish historical memories of the Ottoman deportations of Armenians featured Turks who claimed that not only were there were no massacres of Armenians during that time, but that many Turks provided the fleeing Armenian refugees with food, milk and doctors for their long journeys.

Groupthink

1. Journalists, more notably in TV, work to their own agreed-upon criteria and seem to be oblivious to what the wider public truly want and need. They don't directly gage public reaction to their work on a regular basis. They don't ask for feedback and they certainly don't take into consideration the popular sentiment towards the news writ large which is now largely cynical. The physical newsroom is an insular and restricted space. Security gates and

barriers keep the general public out. Whole parts of it are rendered dark and windowless for both privacy and studio lighting reasons. Key decision-makers at the higher managerial level are unknown and are difficult for the public to contact—let alone for employees. As resources dwindle and newsrooms become further understaffed—the veritable eyes and ears of the organization in the outside world become further handicapped.

News Affective Disorder (NAD)

1. While hosting the opening ceremonies of the 2016 Rio Olympics, former CBC News anchor Peter Mansbridge offered much sombre news-related commentary about the participating nations as they marched into the stadium—far too much for a sporting event in some viewers' opinion.
2. One particularly intense week of news coverage in late August 2015 triggered emotional crises in a few of my newsroom colleagues. That week, scores of African migrants died at sea trying to get to Europe and a Virginia TV reporter and her cameraman were shot during a live broadcast by their disgruntled colleague who later shot himself.

ACKNOWLEDGMENTS

Special thanks to Denise Winn for her edit of this work. To Holly Worton for her plethora of self-publishing advice. I'm also grateful to Ken Dodd, John Bell and Ivan Tyrrell for their insights and feedback on content. Thanks to Michel Vrana for the cover design. Also thanks to Maria Hypponen, Colleen Nicholson, Lori Henry, Laura Bain, Andrew Boden, Ronit Novak and Carolyn Forde.

NOTES

ix, **an accurate picture of the world, would fall away**: Greg Jackson, "Vicious Cycles: Theses on a philosophy of news," in *Harper's Magazine* (online), January 8, 2020. https://harpers.org/archive/2020/01/vicious-cycles-theses-on-a-philosophy-of-news/

xi, **not the child of his ancestors**: Ibn Khaldun, *The Muqaddimah: An Introduction to History*, Translated by Franz Rosenthal. New York: Pantheon, 1958, Vol 2, p. 318.

PREFACE

xvi, **After Eating Marmot**: Jack Guy & Bilegdemberel Gansukh, "Teenage Boy Dies of Bubonic Plague after Eating Marmot," CNN (online), July 15, 2020. https://www.cnn.com/2020/07/15/asia/mongolia-plague-death-scli-intl

xvi, **Amputated To Relieve Pain**: "Bangladesh 'Tree Man' wants hands amputated to relieve pain," CTV News (online), June 24, 2019. https://www.ctvnews.ca/health/bangladesh-tree-man-wants-hands-amputated-to-relieve-pain-1.4479724

xvi, **Sparks Online Frenzy**: "Greta Thunberg Look-Alike In Yukon Gold Rush Photo Sparks Online Frenzy," CBC News (online), November 22, 2019. https://www.cbc.ca/news/canada/north/greta-thunberg-photo-klondike-1.5368901

xvii, **From Woman's Tonsil**: Amy Woodycat, "Doctors Remove Live Worm From Woman's Tonsil," CNN (online), July 14, 2020. https://www.cnn.com/2020/07/14/health/throat-worm-japan-intl-scli/index.html

xvii, **Feces At Tim Hortons Staff**: "Woman detained after video appears to show her throwing own feces at Tim Hortons staff," CBC News (online), May 16, 2018. https://www.cbc.ca/news/canada/british-columbia/tim-hortons-poop-throwing-1.46658

PART I: VEILS OF DISTORTION

p.3 **even when no fire ensued**: Idries Shah, *The Dermis Probe*. London: Octagon Books, 1980, p. 59.

THE NEWS AS DISTORTION

p.5 **information disseminated under the guise of news reporting**: Anita Singh, 'Cuffing season' and 'Corbynmania' are named Words of the Year by Collins Dictionary," *The Telegraph* (online), 2 November 2017. https://www. telegraph.co.uk/news/2017/11/02/cuffing-season-corbynmania-named-words-year-collins-dictionary/

p.5 **otherwise turned back the minute-hand**: John Mecklin, Ed. "A new abnormal: It is still 2 minutes to midnight," 2019 *Doomsday Clock Statement, Science and Security Board*, Bulletin of the Atomic Scientists. https://thebulletin. org/doomsday-clock/2019-doomsday-clock-statement/

p.6 **similar to yelling 'boo' at a sports game**: Michael P. Lynch, "Do We Really Understand 'Fake News'?" *New York Times* (online), September 23, 2019. https://www.nytimes.com/2019/09/23/opinion/fake-news.html

p.6 **those who were largely pro-Trump in orientation**: Alex Fox, "Majority of Americans were not exposed to 'fake news' in 2016 U.S. election, Twitter study suggests," in *Science* (online), January 24, 2019. https://www.sciencemag. org/news/2019/01/majority-americans-were-not-exposed-fake-news-2016-us-election-twitter-study-suggests

And

"Less than you think: Prevalence and predictors of fake news dissemination on Facebook," by Andrew Guess, Jonathan Nagler, and Joshua Tucker, in *Science Advances*, 09 Jan 2019: Vol. 5, no. 1. https://advances.sciencemag.org/content/5/1/eaau4586

p.6 **something far louder and more dangerous," he says**: Joshua Yaffa, "Is Russian Meddling as Dangerous as We Think?" in *The New Yorker* (online), September 14, 2020.

WHY WE'RE DUPES FOR NEWS

p.9 **to tell you what you need to act on next**: Robert Ornstein and Ted Dewan, *MindReal: How the Mind Creates its Own Virtual Reality*. Boston: Malor Books, 2008, p. 136.

p.11 **We compare relative differences between stimuli**: Ibid, p. 115.

p.11 **in the demand for elephant ivory**: "What is the impact of China's Ivory Ban?" in World Wildlife Fund (WWF) website. See https://www.wwf.org.uk/updates/what-impact-chinas-ivory-ban

p.11 **the first Latin American country to entirely eradicate malaria**: Lin Taylor, "Paraguay declared malaria free amid concerns the disease rising again," Reuters (online), June 11, 2018. https://www.reuters.com/article/us-paraguay-malaria-health/paraguay-declared-malaria-free-amid-concerns-the-disease-rising-again-idUSKBN1J7256

THE FILTER

p.13 **this idiosyncratic condensation of the world out there**: Jackson, *Harper's Magazine*, (online).

p.15 **based on values and based on frames**: David Murray, Joel Schwartz, S. Robert Lichter, *It Ain't Necessarily So: How the Media Remake Our Picture of Reality*. New York: Penguin, 2002, p. 6.

p.17 **into crime reporters and war correspondents**: Steven Pinker, *Enlightenment Now: The Case for Reason, Science, Humanism, and Progress*. New York: Viking, 2018, p. 41.

p.19 **455 segments about the Stormy Daniels scandal**: Adam Johnson, "MSNBC has done 455 Stormy Daniels segments in the last year — but none on U.S. war in Yemen," in *Salon* (online), July 25, 2018. https://www.salon.com/2018/07/25/msnbc-has-done-455-stormy-daniels-segments-in-the-last-year-but-none-on-the-war-in-yemen/

EXAGGERATION

p.20 **can only exist as relative to something else**: Iain McGilchrist in an interview with Mark Tyrrell, YouTube, "It's Impossible to Overrate the Importance of Context", 8 June 2020. https://www.youtube.com/watch?v=G5rcZJObnbA

p.23 **must infest all raw fish everywhere**: "Doctors warn sushi-eaters of parasite in raw fish," CTV News (online), May 12, 2017. http://www.ctvnews.ca/health/doctors-warn-sushi-eaters-of-parasite-in-raw-fish-1.3410982#

p.24 **fired up by excessive news coverage?**: "The driver who killed the Humboldt Broncos received too harsh a sentence," by Parker Donham, *National Post* (online), December 30, 2019. https://nationalpost.com/opinion/opinion-the-driver-who-killed-the-humboldt-broncos-received-too-harsh-of-a-sentence

p.25 **let kids roam around their neighbourhoods unsupervised."**: Jonathan Haidt & Greg Lukianoff, *The Coddling of the American Mind: How Good Intentions and Bad Ideas Are Setting Up a Generation for Failure*. New York: Penguin, 2018, p. 166.

p.25 **are among the rarest of crimes**: Ibid.

p.26 **at a time when crime levels have generally plummeted**: Ibid. p. 167.

p.26 **thought to be lax with monitoring their children**: Kim Brooks, "Motherhood in the Age of Fear" in the *New York Times* (online), July 27, 2018. https://www.nytimes.com/2018/07/27/opinion/sunday/motherhood-in-the-age-of-fear.html?

p.27 **in Iranian Custody but Crew Will be Returned 'Promptly.'"**: Lolita C. Baldor, "Two US Navy boats in Iran custody, crew to be returned 'promptly'" Associated Press appearing in the *Christian Science Monitor* (online), January 12, 2013. https://www.csmonitor.com/USA/Foreign-Policy/2016/

0112/Two-US-Navy-boats-in-Iran-custody-crew-to-be-returned-promptly

p.28 exaggerated and inaccurate online headlines: See AJ Plus English (AJ+) https://www.facebook.com/ajplusenglish/videos/470056523135860/

p.29 unless you were rolling around in the plant," the man says: See "Giant hogweed plant that can cause burns and blindness spreading in Canada", The Canadian Press appearing in *Toronto Star* (online), Wednesday August 9, 2017. https://www.thestar.com/news/canada/2017/08/09/giant-hogweed-plant-that-can-cause-burns-and-blindness-spreading-in-canada.html

WHO DOESN'T LOVE A GOOD STORY?: HOW WE ARE HARDWIRED FOR NARRATIVE

p.30 makes us confuse induced emotions with knowledge: Chris Hedges, "'Fake News' in America: Homegrown, and Far From New," in *Truthdig*, December 19, 2016. https://www.truthdig.com/articles/fake-news-in-america-homegrown-and-far-from-new/

p.32 is embedded in the American psyche...": Murray, Schwartz & Lichter, p. 188.

p.38 when we should be learning from it.": Matthew Syed, *Black Box Thinking: The Surprising Truth About Success*. London: John Murray, 2015, p. 246.

p.38 **"mass-printed by-products of the narrative fallacy."**: Ibid p. 250.

p.38 **Barack Obama and Hillary Clinton for "creating" ISIS**: Tal Kopan, "Donald Trump: I meant that Obama founded ISIS, literally," on CNN (online), August 12, 2016. https://www.cnn.com/2016/08/11/politics/donald-trump-hugh-hewitt-obama-founder-isis/index.html

p.38 **helped create the ISIS phenomenon**: John Zada and John Bell, "Who to Blame for ISIL?" in Al Jazeera English (online), January 14, 2016. https://www.aljazeera.com/indepth/opinion/2016/01/blame-isil-160111121327150.html

p.40 **rest upon a likely villain who had suspect intentions."**: Murray, Schwartz, & Lichter, p. 188.

'THE ARGUMENT CULTURE'

p.41 **that will permit truly new understanding**: Deborah Tannen, *The Argument Culture*. New York: Virago Press, 1998, p. 297.

p.41 **behind the gym and beat the hell out of him."'**: Cleve R. Wootson Jr., "Trump and Biden are both openly fantasizing about who would win in a fistfight" in *The Washington Post* (online), March 22, 2018. https://www.washingtonpost.com/news/powerpost/wp/2018/03/21/joe-biden-cant-stop-talking-about-beating-up-donald-trump/

p.44 **irreconcilable principles continually at war.":** Tannen, p. 292.

THE OBJECTIVITY MYTH

p.47 **Because there are always more than two sides**: Idries Shah, *Reflections*, London: Idries Shah Foundation, 2014, p. 57

p.47 **or strives to report, "objective" truth**: Nick Davies, *Flat Earth News: An Award-winning Reporter Exposes Falsehood, Distortion and Propaganda in the Global Media*. London: Vintage, p. 111.

p.48 **quick copy with which no one will quarrel.":** Davies, p. 133.

IT'S ALL JOURNALESE TO ME

p.50 **can be very adept at hiding the truth**: Dan Brown, *The Lost Symbol*, New York: Doubleday, 2009, p. 196.

p.52 **Police Squad Helps Dog Bite Victim**: Philip Howard, *The Press Gang: The World in Journalese*, London: The Institute for Cultural Research, Monograph Series No. 40, 2000, p. 10.

p.52 **Eighth Army Push Bottles Up Germans:** Ibid.

p.52 **Child Teaching Expert To Speak:** Ibid.

p.52 **Woman Better After Being Thrown From High Rise**: Ibid.

p.52 **Solar System Expected To Be Back In Operation**: *Libertyville Herald*, March 15, 1978.

p.52 **Drunk Gets Nine Months In Violin Case**: *The Lethbridge Herald*, October 30, 1976.

p.52 **referred to the virus as the "deadly coronavirus."**: Erick Marcisano, "Trump urges Florida to welcome cruise ship with deadly coronavirus outbreak," Reuters via *Globe and Mail* (online), March 31, 2020. https://www.theglobeandmail.com/world/article-trump-urges-florida-to-welcome-cruise-ship-with-deadly-coronavirus/

p.52 **commuter car activity as "deadly traffic."**: Al Tompkins, "How newsrooms can tone down their coronavirus coverage while still reporting responsibly," in *Poynter* (online), March 4, 2020. https://www.poynter.org/reporting-editing/2020/how-newsrooms-can-tone-down-their-coronavirus-coverage-while-still-reporting-responsibly/

p.54 **the regime's bombardment, siege and starvation…**: "The Islamic State Through the Looking Glass," first published in the *The Arabist*, republished by the International Crisis Group (ICG) online. https://www.crisisgroup.org/global/islamic-state-through-looking-glass

COLOURED BY NUMBERS

p.55 **never find out the time in a clock shop.'**: Idries Shah, *Observations*, London: Idries Shah Foundation, 2019, p. 130.

p.55 **refuted or attenuated over time**: Kelly Crowe, "It's news, but is it true?" CBC News (online), Oct 05, 2012. https://www.cbc.ca/news/health/it-s-news-but-is-it-true-1.1282472

p.59 **whether it is organic or not**: Brad Plumer, "Is organic food any healthier? Most scientists are still skeptical," in *Vox*, June 5, 2015. https://www.vox.com/2014/7/16/5899347/organic-produce-debate-healthier-more-nutritious

p.59 **stay indoors more often and get less sunshine**: Christopher Labos MD, "The Link Between Vitamin D and Alzheimer's," The Office for Science and Society (online), McGill University, Oct 3, 2019. https://mcgill.ca/oss/article/health-nutrition/link-between-vitamin-d-and-alzheimers

p.60 **also be more willing to contemplate divorce."**: Oliver Burkeman, "Are you married to the right person – and does it matter?" in *The Guardian* (online), Nov. 16, 2018. https://www.theguardian.com/lifeandstyle/2018/nov/16/marriage-cohabit-successful-commitment-compatible-oliver-burkeman

p.60 **No more, no less."**: Murray, Schwartz and Lichter, p. 9.

p.61 **A 2017 article in *Vox* does just that**: Brian Resnick, "Study: half of the studies you read about in the news are wrong," in *Vox*, March 3, 2017. https://www.vox.com/science-and-health/2017/3/3/14792174/half-scientific-studies-news-are-wrong

FROM PR TO PROPAGANDA

p.63 **because it is designed to serve an interest.":** Davies, p. 89.

p.63 **lending his celebrity presence to the show**: CBC News Network YouTube Channel, March 20, 2018. https://www.youtube.com/watch?v=5LFFqJ2t0YE

p.63 **to launch her own food brand**: CBC News Network television broadcast, August 9, 2017.

p.64 **who was looming somewhere in the background**: Robyn Urback, "The media should know better but we keep falling for Trudeau's PR," in CBC News (online) May 25, 2017. https://www.cbc.ca/news/opinion/trudeau-photo-ops-1.4130208

p.66 **including in many mainstream news organizations**: See Loch K. Johnson, *America's Secret Power: The CIA in a Democratic Society*. Oxford: Oxford University Press, 1995, pp. 22, 185.

p.66 **foreign news media in the late 1980s**: Scott Shane, "Russia Isn't the Only One Meddling in Elections. We Do It, Too." *New York Times* (online) February 17, 2018. https://www.nytimes.com/2018/02/17/sunday-review/russia-isnt-the-only-one-meddling-in-elections-we-do-it-too.html

p.66 **a pillar of its covert propaganda operations**: Nick McKenzie, Paul Sakkal, and Grace Tobin, "Defecting Chinese spy offers information trove to Australian government," in *The Age* (online), November 23, 2019. https://amp.theage.com.au/national/defecting-chinese-spy-offers-information-trove-to-australian-government-20191122-p53d1l.html?

p.66 **influence a country's policies through the press."**: Adam Taylor, "Before 'fake news,' there was Soviet 'disinformation,'" in *The Washington Post* (online), Nov 26, 2016. https://www.washingtonpost.com/news/worldviews/wp/2016/11/26/before-fake-news-there-was-soviet-disinformation/

p.67 **and continues to have numerous proponents**: Yaffa, *The New Yorker* (online).

p.67 **the statue came from a U.S. Marine colonel."**: Jeff Cohen, *Cable News Confidential: My Misadventures in Corporate Media*. Sausalito: PoliPoint Press, 2006, p. 190.

p.67 **was a relatively inconsequential jihadist**: Davies, p. 206.

PART II: THE NEWS FACTORY

p.73 **is in fact an element in the machine**: Norbert Wiener, *The Human Use of Human Beings*. London: Sphere Books, 1968, p. 161.

THE MAN BEHIND THE CURTAIN

p.75 **Is that an Emperor at all?'**: Idries Shah, *Reflections*, London: Idries Shah Foundation, 2014, p. 148.

'CHURNALISM'

p.78 **some things need to be done slowly**: Chris Ross, *Tunnel Visions: Journeys of an Underground Philosopher*. London: Fourth Estate, 2001, p. 66.

CAPTURE AND HOLD

p.83 **which it sells back to advertisers**: Tim Wu, *The Attention Merchants: The Epic Scramble to Get Inside Our Heads*. New York: Knopf, 2016.

THE ERRORS OF OUR WAYS

p.86 **largely unchecked second-hand material**: Davies, p. 60.

p. 86 **the upper peninsula of Michigan in Canada**: Fox News broadcast with host Sean Hannity, November 18th 2020.

p.87 **the young girl later admitted to making it up**: See "Toronto girl's family 'deeply sorry' for untrue hijab-cutting story," The Canadian Press in Globe and Mail (online), January 18, 2018. https://www.theglobeandmail.com/news/toronto/toronto-girls-family-deeply-sorry-for-untrue-hijab-cutting-story-reports/article37653871/

p.87 **reporting errors made by that unit over time**: Sydney Ember & Michael M. Grynbaum "At CNN, Retracted Story Leaves an Elite Reporting Team Bruised", in *New York Times* (online), Sept. 5, 2017. https://www.nytimes.com/2017/09/05/business/media/cnn-retraction-trump-scaramucci.html?

p.88 **a United Arab Emirates publication called Emirates 24/7**: Muna Ahmed, "Dad lets daughter die, rather than be touched by 'strange' rescuer," in *Emirates 24/7*, August 9, 2015. https://www.emirates247.com/news/emirates/dad-lets-daughter-die-rather-than-be-touched-by-strange-rescuer-2015-08-09-1.599613

p.88 **being reported as news, took place back in 1996**: "Mail Online and Telegraph's Dubai drowning tale is old news," in *The Guardian* (online), August 11, 2015. https://www.theguardian.com/media/mediamonkey-blog/2015/aug/11/mail-online-telegraphs-dubai-drowning

And

Lubna Hamdan, "Case of father refusing to save his drowning daughter at a Dubai beach is nearly 20 years old," in *Arabian Business* (online), August 13, 2015. https://www.arabianbusiness.com/case-of-father-refusing-save-his-drowning-daughter-at-dubai-beach-is-nearly-20-years-old-602581.html

DUMB AND DUMBER

p.90 **it is there for our amusement and pleasure**: Neil Postman, *Amusing Ourselves to Death: Public Discourse in the Age of Show Business*. New York: Penguin Books, 2005, p. 87.

p.90 **the product of a for-profit entertainment industry? Yes."**: Jackson, *Harper's Magazine* (online)

p.90 **salacious gossip than an important event**: "Two Catholic nuns left Italy to do mission work in Africa. When they returned, they were pregnant," in *The National Post* (online), November 6, 2019.

p.92 **Obamas ratcheted over 24 million American viewers**: Michael O'Connell, "CBS' Stormy Sitdown Has '60 Minutes' at Decade High, Topping 22 Million Viewers," in *Billboard* (online), March 26, 2018. https://www.billboard.com/articles/news/8261239/stormy-daniels-60-minutes-ratings-22-million-viewers p.93 **wondering why this was a story**: CBC News Network television broadcast, Tuesday February 11, 2020.

p.93 **or Whitney Houston's daughter's ex-boyfriend**: "Ex-boyfriend of Whitney Houston's late daughter dead at 30," in Associated Press, published on CBC News (online), Jan 1, 2020. https://www.cbc.ca/news/entertainment/whitney-houston-bobbi-kristina-brown-nick-gordon-death-1.5412587

p.94 **can nowadays sometimes wake up to**: CBC News Network television broadcast, July 12, 2017.

TRUMPING THE REAL STORY

p.96 **this was the story of a lifetime."**: Jackson, *Harper's Magazine*, (online)

p.97 **but it's damn good for CBS."**: Paul Bond, "Leslie Moonves on Donald Trump: "It May Not Be Good for America, but It's Damn Good for CBS", in *Hollywood Reporter*, Feb 29, 2016. http://www.hollywoodreporter.com/news/leslie-moonves-donald-trump-may-871464

p.97 **right now, Donald Trump dominates."**: Joe Pompeo, "It's Our Job to Call Them Out: Inside the Trump Gold Rush at CNN," in *Vanity Fair* (online), Nov. 1, 2018. https://www.vanityfair.com/news/2018/11/inside-the-trump-gold-rush-at-cnn

And

John Bowden, "CNN boss: If we break away from Trump coverage 'the audience goes away'," in *The Hill* (online), Nov. 1, 2018. https://thehill.com/homenews/media/414390-cnn-boss-if-we-break-from-trump-coverage-the-audience-goes-away

p.98 **or by the President himself**: Robby Mook, "The Great Distractor," in the *New York Times* (online), August 7, 2018. https://www.nytimes.com/2018/08/07/opinion/donald-trump-the-great-distractor.html

FEW EXPERTS HERE

p.100 **surprisingly little about many things**: Howard, p. 8.

p.100 **something about the issue being discussed."**: Chapman Pincher, *Inside Story: A Documentary About the Pursuit of Power*. London: Sidgwick & Jackson, 1981. Quoted in Idries Shah, *The Natives are Restless: Adventures Among the English - and Others*. London: Octagon Books, 1988, p. 173.

p.102 **to sustain human life there**: Caleb A. Scharf, "Death on Mars," in *Scientific American* (online), January 20, 2020. https://blogs.scientificamerican.com/life-unbounded/death-on-mars1/

p.102 **those issues helped create societal angst**: Davies, pp. 9–12, 26–27.

p.103 **and thus don't make for a reliable weapon**: Murray, Schwartz & Lichter, pp. 197–212.

p.103 **caused little damage, either physical and radiological**: Davies pp. 43–44.

p.104 **ran on the CBC News website**: Bethany Lindsay, "'It blows my mind': How B.C. destroys a key natural wildfire defence every year", in CBC News (online), Nov 17, 2018. https://www.cbc.ca/news/canada/british-columbia/it-blows-my-mind-how-b-c-destroys-a-key-natural-wildfire-defence-every-year-1.4907358

p.104 **factors in the other print and online media**: "How to Break Western Canada's Accelerating Cycle of Wild-fires," Editorial, *Globe and Mail* (online), June 5, 2019. https://www.theglobeandmail.com/opinion/editorials/article-how-to-break-western-canadas-accelerating-cycle-of-wildfires/

And

Matt Simon, "The Age of Flames Is Consuming California," in *Wired* (online), October 24, 2019. https://www.wired.com/story/kincade-fire/

VIGILANCE MISDIRECTED

p.105 **ever further down the same path**: Iain McGilchrist, *The Master and His Emissary: The Divided Brain* *and the Making of the Western World*. New Haven: Yale University Press, 2009, p. xxiv.

GROUPTHINK: WHEN NO ONE SPEAKS UP

p.114 **which he admitted was a poor decision**: Tara Deschamps, "'I am extremely sorry': Ottawa Senators Uber driver discusses video," *Toronto Star* (online), November 18, 2018. https://www.thestar.com/sports/hockey/2018/11/18/i-am-extremely-sorry-ottawa-senators-uber-driver-discusses-video.html

p.114 **by people when making collective decisions**: See Carol S. Dweck, *Mindset: The New Psychology of Success*. New York: Ballantine, 2006, pp. 134–136.

NEWS AFFECTIVE DISORDER (NAD): THE COST TO OUR HEALTH

p.116 **by inadvertence, making people crazy**: Michael Enright, "Michael's essay: The rapid pace of news is leaving us exhausted and depressed," CBC News (online), June 15, 2018. https://www.cbc.ca/radio/thesundayedition/the-sunday-edition-june-17-2018-1.4692469/michael-s-essay-the-rapid-pace-of-news-is-leaving-us-exhausted-and-depressed-1.4703966?

p.116 **to be the first to herald ill**: Burton Stevenson, *Stevenson's Book of Proverbs, Maxims and Familiar Phrases*. London: Routledge and Kegan Paul, 1949, p.1168.

p.116 **helping to make us physically and psychologically unwell**: Ibid.

PART III: WHAT TO DO

p.121 **the former can ruin nations."**: Alain De Botton, *The News: A User's Manual.* Oxford: Signal, 2014, p. 75.

HIGH STAKES

p.130 **calls "cognitive diversity," or diverse thinking**: Matthew Syed, Rebel Ideas: *The Power of Diverse Thinking.* London: John Murray, 2020.

p.132 **the illusions which flood our experience**: Boorstin, p. 3

p.136 **in the brief time still allotted to us."**: De Botton, p. 255.

ENDNOTES

p.137 **Iraq being the most memorable but by no means only example**: Glen Greenwald, "CNN Journalists Resign: Latest Example of Media Recklessness on the Russia Threat," *The Intercept*, June 27, 2017. https://theintercept.com/2017/06/27/cnn-journalists-resign-latest-example-of-media-recklessness-on-the-russia-threat/

p.138 **absolutely safe for habitation and development**: See the website for The National Academies of Sciences Engineering Medicine, April 24, 2009. http://www8.nationalacademies.org/onpinews/newsitem.aspx?RecordID=12647

p.138 **uncertainty inherent in early biomedical studies."**: Brian Resnick, 2017.

p.139 **as they did his presidential predecessors**: Musa al-Gharbi, "The New York Times' obsession with Trump, quantified," in *Columbia Journalism Review* (online), November 13, 2019. https://www.cjr.org/covering_the_election/new-york-times-trump.php

p.140 **and none were Iranian-American**: Tyler Monroe and Lis Power, "Here are all the people who have been on weekday cable news to talk about Iran," in Media Matters for America (online), January 15, 2020. https://www.mediamatters.org/cable-news/here-are-all-people-who-have-been-weekday-cable-news-talk-about-iran

p.140 **found across the autistic spectrum,"**: See http://www.caetextia.com

p.140 **including possibly, if inadvertently, members of ISIS**: Michael Stevens, "Islamic State: Where does jihadist group get its support?" BBC News (online), 1 September, 2014. https://www.bbc.com/news/world-middle-east-29004253

And

Tom Keatinge, "Why Qatar is the focus of terrorism claims," BBC News (online), 12 June 2017. https://www.bbc.com/news/world-middle-east-40246734

p.140 **with food, milk and doctors for their long journeys**: Al Jazeera English television broadcast, April 24, 2015.

p.141 **in some viewers' opinion**: John Doyle, "It's about time: We've put up with Mansbridge and his pompous ilk for too long," in *Globe and Mail*, Sept 6, 2016. https://www.theglobeandmail.com/arts/television/its-about-time-weve-put-up-with-mansbridge-and-his-pompous-ilk-for-too-long/article31720560/

INDEX

ABOUT THE AUTHOR

John Zada is a writer, photographer and journalist who has worked as a television news writer for both CBC News Network and Al Jazeera English. He is also the author of the book *In the Valleys of the Noble Beyond: In Search of the Sasquatch*. His articles have appeared in the *Globe & Mail, Toronto Star, Explore, CBC, Al Jazeera, BBC, Los Angeles Review of Books*, and elsewhere. John lives in Toronto, Canada.

A REQUEST

If you enjoyed this book, please review it on Amazon and Goodreads.

Reviews are an author's best friend.

To stay in touch with John Zada, and to hear about his upcoming releases before anyone else, please sign up for his mailing list at:

www.johnzada.com

And to follow him on social media, please go to any of the following links:

twitter.com/senor_adaz
instagram.com/johnzada
linkedin.com/in/johnzada
goodreads.com/john_zada
facebook.com/johnzada

CPSIA information can be obtained
at www.ICGtesting.com
Printed in the USA
FSHW020503160421
80541FS

9 781777 357108